MYLES

Portraits of Brian O'Nolan

MYLES

PORTRAITS OF

BRIAN O'NOLAN

Edited by Timothy O'Keeffe

MARTIN BRIAN
& O'KEEFFE
LONDON

First published in 1973
by Martin Brian & O'Keeffe Ltd
37 Museum Street London WC1

ISBN 0 85616 150 0

This collection
© Martin Brian & O'Keeffe Ltd 1973

Printed in Great Britain by
Latimer Trend & Company Ltd
Plymouth

FOR EVELYN

FOR EVELYN

Contents

Illustrations

A Poem from the Irish

(twelfth-century, anonymous)

My hand has a pain from writing,
Not steady the sharp tool of my craft,
Its slender beak spews bright ink—
A beetle-dark shining draught.

Streams of wisdom of white God
From my fair-brown, fine hand sally,
On the page they splash their flood
In ink of the green-skinned holly.

My little dribbly pen stretches
Across the great white paper plain,
Insatiable for splendid riches—
That is why my hand has pain!

BRIAN O'NOLAN

The following abbreviations are used in the text:

AS2B—*At Swim-Two-Birds*

FK —*Faustus Kelly*

CL —'Cruiskeen Lawn'

HL —*The Hard Life*

DA —*The Dalkey Archive*

3P —*The Third Policeman*

BoM —*The Best of Myles*

Preface

THE origins of this book derive from a number of points of view, though they unite in the belief that Brian O'Nolan was a man of brave temperament and intellect, beside being an outstanding writer. His younger brother, Kevin O Nolan, writes of him in the context of their uncommon family. I used to laugh long and hard at Brinsley in *At Swim-Two-Birds* long before I met Niall Sheridan, the begetter: I still do. Through his eyes we see something of the remarkable student, a young man for whom the world held what might be called the incandescence of comedy in its vitals.

John Garvin and Jack White concern themselves with Brian O'Nolan's two most 'significant' public works, the former as civil servant and the latter, more famously, as Myles na Gopaleen, the wit and scourge of the Plain People of Ireland in the columns of the *Irish Times*. J. C. C. Mays writes as a literary scholar and it is appropriate to include here his evaluation of Brian O'Nolan's writings; up to now we have had miscellaneous attempts at an estimation but nothing so sustained and just. Another book, as they say, could be written to illustrate other facets of Brian O'Nolan's character and activities, but a diligent researcher can find something of these in other sources. I count the fact that Patrick Kavanagh wept at losing him as a worthy memorial.

At Swim-Two-Birds had for a long time acquired that curious mark of fame, of being the most-stolen book of its time. As the first edition appeared to sink slowly to oblivion, from that mire large bubbles of pure nitrous oxide began slowly, then more vigorously, to break to the surface. In the mid-50's I had tried to have it re-issued but did not succeed in doing so until I changed publishing horses in 1959. Its reappearance and recognition—despite various denigrations of his own—were welcome to Brian O'Nolan, partly, I think, because he was a man private and scholarly, who had—perhaps to test himself—become a public and controversial figure in a comparatively small city. He was open therefore to personal pressures and hostilities in a way that a writer in London, say, or Paris, generally is not. It is notorious what tolls are exacted in spirit of a writer by the journalistic processes and it must have seemed like a return to fresher days and more ample horizons when his first masterpiece made its belated new début.

I knew Brian O'Nolan only in these latter days, and published his later books. Anyone with the price of a newspaper could still have Myles na Gopaleen with his morning egg and rasher but at last it was possible to keep a copy of *At Swim* on one's shelf, unchained. The man who had welcomed R. M. Smyllie's attention would recognise that his greater achievement lay between the limits of the two covers he alone had marked out. By nature he was more fit for private fame than the readier laughter of the street or bar. Yet laughter is forever in short supply and in his columns we see the constituents of his perfected writing. One of the tests that I should like to set for any potential thesis-writer is to call for an analysis, at de Selbean footnote length perhaps, of the comedy of Myles's description of a particular Dublin flower trough as 'the tomb of the unknown gurrier'.

What, finally, may Brian O'Nolan yet have to say about the eventual appearance of *The Third Policeman*? For a man who gave the terror of death a classic expression so many years ago, can even his own death inhibit him now?

January 1973   TIMOTHY O'KEEFFE

KEVIN O NOLAN

The First Furlongs

MAN's preoccupation with man is nothing new. But the increasing extent of that preoccupation is alarming. The man who knows only that Dante is a racehorse may be a two-way loser, but in another sense he gains. He will not become the prisoner of another man's life, uncovering his tracks, his interests, even acquiring some of the things he once owned. That takes time. You could lose your life that way. It may be objected, and rightly, that the study of mankind, of other men, is an enrichment of one's life. And if the maxim that life is short, art long, has any meaning away from its original context, it must be this, that art is a sort of permanence won from passing and perishable life. Art and life are thus related but their relationship is not to be explored in a sentence.

Biography flourishes partly at least because people feel that a man's life may throw some light on his works. Ancient biographers went so far as to construct suitable lives from the works where nothing was known of the authors. Such lives could add nothing to knowledge, and I doubt if even genuine lives can aid with certainty the understanding of a man's work. It is this doubt that makes me reluctant to embark even on this short biographical essay of my brother, Brian O'Nolan, known to readers under his own name, and by the pen-names, Flann O'Brien and Myles na Gopaleen. I am further inhibited by the subject's own view of biography, expressed briefly in an article of his column, 'Cruiskeen Lawn'. Commenting on a biography of Shaw he wrote: 'Like the entire breed of biographies, it is too devout. It was precisely this sort of devotional literature, piling mountain-high during Victoria's

13

reign (all uncover, please) that caused the equally distorted portraits of latter-day debunkers. Biography is the lowest form of letters and is atrophied by the subject's own censorship, conscious or otherwise.' The present essay, however, may be useful in outlining the subject's early life in a factual manner. The whole family had the same upbringing, more or less, and a certain community of experience.*

Brian was born on the 5th October, 1911, the third of a family of twelve. The full roll-call is Gearóid, Ciarán, Brian, Róisin, Fergus, Kevin, Maeve, Nessa, Nuala, Sheila, Michael and Niall. The father was Michael Victor Nolan, whose family came from near Omagh in Tyrone. Some account of that family is given by his brother, the late Rev. Gerald O'Nolan, who was for many years Professor of Irish in St Patrick's College, Maynooth.† Michael, Gerald, another brother, Fergus, and a fourth, Peter, a Carmelite priest, were all well versed in Latin and Greek. Michael, Gerald and Fergus also showed an early enthusiasm for the Irish language and its revival. Gerald and Fergus wrote in that language, including jointly a book of short stories, which they also published in English under the title *Intrusions*, Fergus also producing a play, *A Royal Alliance*, which the Abbey Theatre produced in 1920. Michael had early acquired a thorough knowledge of Irish. It was by no means dead in Tyrone in his youth: one of his life-long friends, Dr Seamas O'Kelly, was actually a native speaker of Tyrone Irish. Michael, however, turned to the more vital Donegal tradition and became a close friend of Seamas Mac a' Bhaird, one-time king of Tory Island and a very good story-teller. Thus while Michael taught Irish widely in the years before his marriage in 1906, he did not, as far as I know, write in Irish. At the time of his death in 1937 among his papers there was found the typescript of a book in English —a detective novel—which was highly praised by Collins's reader.

* I am indebted to my brother, Ciarán, who has kindly allowed me to use a series of articles in Irish (which he wrote and published in *Inniu*) on the family background and on Brian's early life up to his entering University. In the course of preparing those articles he confirmed by documents and otherwise many dates and facts which otherwise would still await investigation.

† In *Beatha Duine a Thoil*, an autobiography written in Irish.

The accompanying correspondence, which dated from the period of the First World War, showed that Collins had made an offer of publication but Michael's agent had strongly advised against acceptance because of the small sum offered.*

One might suppose that this side of the family provided Brian with his learned and literary background, if one did not know the mother's side.

The mother was Agnes Gormley, daughter of a Tyrone man, John Gormley, who settled in Strabane and established a business there. His family was also large, but, as we ourselves grew up, we came into close contact with those members of it who remained in Strabane. We knew and occasionally met Tom and Jack who had left Strabane. But the mother's brothers, Joe and Eugene, and her sister, Teresa, all of whom remained in the business in Strabane, were very close to us, visited us often wherever we lived, and we spent long periods in Strabane on holidays. It was a second home.

Another brother, George, had gone to Dublin when he was quite young and became a journalist. When our family eventually settled in Dublin, we came into much closer contact with George, and Brian was particularly friendly with him in later days when most of us had grown up. George became something of a legend in the city's journalistic circles and would need a separate essay to himself. Mention of him here calls to mind a small incident which, briefly as I must recount it, must suffice to characterize the Gormleys' command of the crushing retort and their control of laconic utterance which one had to experience to believe. The Gormleys—the mother's family—were well schooled, although lacking the advantage of a university education, if that be considered an advantage. But they were also sufficiently close to a rich unlettered tradition to give them command of a vocabulary and modes of speech not to be found in the ordinary dictionaries. We, as we grew up, with our book-biased training, were constantly delighted at the vividness and economy of language casually practised by our Strabane elders, and at a great range of strange words like

* By a coincidence the Second World War 'killed' Brian's first book, *At Swim-Two-Birds*. It was first published by Longmans in 1939.

'hochle' and 'boke' which seemed more expressive than the ordinary words to be found in books.

However, to return to George, on one occasion he ran into his brother, Eugene, who was on a visit to Dublin from Strabane. He was then mainly, and always remained, a racing journalist. (He once attempted to smuggle under cover of his coat a greyhound through the British Customs, and was heavily fined for his pains.) He invited Eugene, whose interests lie in the local history of Strabane and Tyrone, and who never had any interest in horses, to accompany him to the races at Leopardstown. They set off by taxi in the company of other newspapermen and, by a roundabout course with sundry stops for refreshment, eventually reached Leopardstown. The day was fine and Eugene was left to his own devices. George, who was both reporting the races and also punting, returned from time to time to report that he was doing well. Finally, before the last race, he appeared and pointed to the train, which was steaming at the platform. (The Harcourt Street line at that time ran by the edge of the racecourse and was a favourite means of transport to and from the Leopardstown meetings.) He told Eugene to make a dash for the train as soon as ever the last race finished. This he did, and the two of them managed to secure seats in a carriage. Very soon the train filled up and not only were all seats taken but their carriage like others had four or five standing.

Eugene, in his northern accent began to talk about the day at Leopardstown and George, who had a resonant voice and had never lost his accent, must have appeared to the others present to be a stranger too. At any rate, a man sitting opposite decided to provide some amusement for his fellow travellers on their way to Harcourt Street. He addressed Eugene and asked, 'Is this the first time you gentlemen were at the races?' Eugene didn't answer because, as he told me when I verified the story with him recently, he 'thought the man was drunk!' The man repeated his question in a louder tone and one can only stand back in horror at the idea of anyone including George in such a query, who may be said without much exaggeration to have *invented* racing. At any rate, when the question had been twice asked and a silence had fallen in the carriage, George leaned forward and

1. Strabane: Mourne River and Bridge

2. The O'Nolan House, Tullamore. Brian at the centre

3. Mrs. O'Nolan with Gearóid

said in that clear resonant voice of his: 'It's the first time we were at today's races!'

I have heard this story told a few times and each time there followed a description of the laughter of all present and of the discomfiture of the questioner, who remained silent and red-faced until the terminus was reached. But when I sought Eugene's version of the story, he wrote to say that the man was red-faced from the start—that is why he thought he was drunk! Not only that, but that, following George's reply, there was no laughter but utter silence in the carriage. George had been too smart. Nobody quite knew what to make of him—whether he had uttered a shattering retort, or whether he was a man, perhaps, who should be locked up.

George had been too subtle. Brian also made acid retorts which often failed to explode. He was particularly quick, as some people are, to see the comic irony of situations; others see it when it is pointed out. I remember once my mother talking of another of her brothers, Joe. He was a notable musician in Strabane, a song writer and producer of operas and musical shows. In later life he grew increasingly deaf and my mother was remarking that at that time he was giving much of his time to piano tuition. Brian laughed and commented on the irony of a man teaching the piano when he had all but lost his hearing. My mother did not think it amusing. Perhaps, like the silent keyboard, there was sense in it. Another time I remember Brian commenting with relish on the shattering use a certain Land Commissioner made of his hearing-aid. He would listen carefully for a moment to what somebody was saying and then quietly, while the man was in full spate, turn off his battery!

Michael Victor Nolan and Agnes Gormley were married on the 3rd September, 1906, in the parish church at Murlough, near Strabane. Michael Nolan was then a Customs and Excise Officer and continued to live in Strabane for some years. There, in no. 15 the Bowling Green (on the 5th October, 1911), Brian was born. The family now numbered three boys, Gearóid, Ciarán and Brian, and when the father was transferred to Glasgow the family moved to the suburb of Uddingston. Then followed a return—to Dublin, where the family lived in Inchicore and continued there until the beginning of 1917. Ciarán recalls that on one occasion, when he and Brian were playing in a field near the house, Brian found a small bottle containing a milky fluid which he promptly drank. When his father heard about it, he gave him an emetic which caused Brian to disgorge the fluid with the same promptness as he had ingested it. Whether the bottle had contained Blarney water or something more toxic remains unknown. Possibly the whole family showed the same tendency for sampling unknown substances, for I seem to recall other occasions when the mysterious antidote was hastily got ready. I remember mustard was one of the ingredients.

From Inchicore the next family move was occasioned by the father's promotion to the rank of Surveyor. The work entailed travel and absence from home, and he rented a house in Strabane so that the family could be near the mother's relatives. The house was in Ballycolman Lane, where Strabane spills across the river Mourne by way of the bridge at the head of the town.

The family lived for some years in that house which, by all accounts, was haunted. My mother's family, to judge by various experiences which some of them relate, is somewhat psychic and not unduly disturbed by unnatural happenings. However, the unusual manifestations in the house must have caused some uneasiness, for the father's brother, Peter, a Carmelite priest, visited the house and celebrated Mass in it. The chief occurrences at night-time were the noisy shutting of open windows or the opening of shut windows, although in the morning they appeared not to have been disturbed. Heavy dragging was heard across floors and a bumping noise down the stairs; sometimes also a distinctive noise as of marbles rolled across floor-boards. The sound of sawing was sometimes heard, and sometimes there was a smell of bacon or rashers being cooked.

If my brothers were older at the time I would in retrospect be inclined to regard them as prime suspects in these matters. At a later time any or all of these manifestations could occur naturally any night, as the family had (and still have) the habit of staying up into the small hours, each very likely engaged in his own private (and possibly noisy) pursuit. I remember, for example, much later, when we were living in Blackrock, an occasion when Brian suddenly took to sawing wood and the basement re-echoed to thunderous hammering. Nobody knew what he was up to until the manufacture gradually took shape—a table, rough but serviceable. The legs were strengthened at the top by triangular face-pieces at each corner—something Policeman Mac-Cruiskeen would not have countenanced. When it was finished he asked Gearóid to help him carry it upstairs to his room, which was at the top of the house. That is the table at which *At Swim-Two-Birds* and *The Third Policeman* were written. However, as to the noises in the Ballycolman house, not only were the three brothers not responsible but knowledge of the manifestations was to a large extent successfully kept from them until the family had left the house.

I once asked my mother about these matters, and she remarked that strange things happened by day as well. She said that when anything happened it was of such a kind as not to be alarming at the time. For example, her sister came to the house most evenings from the Gormley house on the other side of the bridge. She would hear the familiar step along a path by the side of the house and then Teresa would appear. One evening she heard the step earlier than usual, but the sister did not come in. Thinking she had stopped for something, my mother went out to investigate. There was no sign of Teresa, nobody. Much later Teresa came as usual. She had not been near the house until then.

Another time, my mother recalled, she was in an inside room when she heard the flap of wings from the kitchen and the scrape of nails on the kitchen table. The sound was perfectly familiar (I hope that is the right word). She kept hens, and, when the kitchen door was open, one or two of them might wander in looking for food. If there was nobody there to shoo them out, they would make bold to forage for themselves. She hurried out to evict the intruder. The kitchen door was not open, there was no hen there. These same hens could never be induced to use the outhouse which was provided for their night shelter. At night, summer and winter, they roosted in the trees.

Ciarán recalls that while they lived in Ballycolman a few efforts were made to give the three boys some schooling. They did not go to any school but a Miss Boyle came to the house for a short spell and later a teacher called Collins. Finally the father attempted to teach them by correspondence, sending each a separate letter with exercises. However, without supervision nothing much was done. When the family next changed house, it was to Tullamore they went, to a house about two miles outside the town. There school was even more out of the question. The result was that these three did not go to school until we moved to Dublin. By that time Brian was almost twelve and Gearóid first appeared at school at an age when most pupils were leaving. They were all at least as far advanced leaving school as anyone else, and it makes one wonder whether the whole school system is a vast fraud operated in the interests of educators. It is possible that the proper time to attend school is when one has retired on pension and can afford the time.

At any rate, for the three eldest of the family formal lessons were minimal and made little impact. The only thing Ciarán can recall is that the visiting teacher read with them an Irish version of *The Children of Lir*. Non-attendance at school was not a consequence of distance or isolation, as I may seem to have implied. The father was a great man for the long walk and from an early age we were all well able to walk long distances. At a later time, in Herbert Place and Blackrock, we were (to our great reluctance) compelled to accompany our father on Sundays on a nine- or ten-mile walk before lunch. I was seven or eight when I was included in this ritual and I can well recall the sinking feeling when, following a superior compass out along the Stillorgan Road with a right turn at Foster Avenue and a gradual veering back to the course of the Dodder, we arrived back at the crossroads at Donnybrook and I realized that we were still half an hour's walk from home. A meal awaited us, the main constituent of which was a joint of the primest midland beef sent to us from Kilbeggan week in week out for twenty years since leaving Tullamore by a good man called Kelly. To an extent Sunday was a predictable day, and such was my own mood at least that I would have cheerfully carved Mr Kelly with his own knives. One man's beef can become another man's beef.

The combination of long Sunday walks and Kilbeggan beef may

have had one favourable consequence in that we were all able, in our unaccompanied outings, to go long distances on foot without fatigue. We might, for example, walk from Herbert Place to Merrion Strand, follow the tide out and, picking our way through shallow and deeper water, our boots hanging around our necks, manage to visit the Pigeon House. Our way home would be different again with possibly a call at Ringsend.

At any rate, to return to Ballycolman, school was as yet in the distant future. The family now numbered six and the mother, what with the knockings and bumpings and the care of the three youngest, must have been forced to leave the seniors to their own devices more often than she would have wished. They were elusive anyway like all children and often absent, up the river-side or somewhere else, bringing themselves up under that reputable lacy fair teacher, Experience. She taught Gearóid one lesson which must have had a strong impact. One day in his probing into the mysteries of aerodynamics he went up on the roof, opened an umbrella and jumped off. He broke his leg.

When the eldest child is a girl, the mother is likely to have at an early stage a helpful and responsible minder for the baby of the family. Unfortunately Róisín, the eldest girl of our family, came only fourth, and the task of baby-minding fell initially on the three eldest boys. They might be required to give notice if the baby was awake or crying, or perhaps to quieten it or put it asleep by gentle agitation when it was in its pram.

It was a task which called for patience if the baby was uneasy, and boys whose minds were occupied with aerodynamics or plain warfare with neighbouring boys had little patience. The prams of that day were high boat-like affairs with exuberant parabolic springs, which could take on a dangerous motion of their own when the pram itself was propelled at speed. Brian in particular was given to this solution— *solvitur currendo*—of running with the pram until the elliptical springs, straining forwards and backwards, brought all to grief. He was often in trouble on this score when we moved to Tullamore, where there was more scope, and I myself, who occupied the hot seat at the time, was the chief victim. Our mother must have looked forward to the night, even in Ballycolman with its noisy but undangerous otherworld troopers.

The move to Tullamore was occasioned by the father's appointment to an area of the midlands with headquarters in the town. He rented a large house called *The Beeches*, at Cappincur, about two miles from Tullamore. He still travelled a good deal and bought a car for the purpose—an Overland. The house was a large solid affair with good gardens and outbuildings. It was open country with fields stretching in all directions. Beside us was our only near neighbour, a family called Daly, who were farmers. I myself remember them with affection because, as soon as ever I got out of the dangerous pram, leaving it to the next tenant, my sister, Maeve, I toddled, aided and abetted by Fergus, as far as Daly's on an independent social call and demanded jelly, which—amazingly—we got. Such trifles hold their place in the memory, the big things are forgotten.

Perhaps it would be more accurate to say that the big things were noted but not understood. Whatever the three eldest brothers made of the War of Independence in Ireland, it meant little to me or Fergus, who was immediately above me in age. I remember that we understood enough to view soldiers with hostility. I recall gazing with Fergus at a pall of smoke in the distance over Tullamore, where some large building had been set on fire. Another time our father brought some of us out in the car to see a huge tree which had been cut down across the road to prevent the passage of Black and Tans. Another day, a Sunday when we were having dinner, a tender full of the same grim-faced visitors stopped on the road in front of the house and some of the soldiers began to take large stones from our wall, no doubt to fill a pit in the road. Gearóid, Ciarán and Brian expressed great indignation but my father told them to stay where they were. Eventually the soldiers left.

Only Róisin went to school during the three or so years we spent in Tullamore. Those who were younger were too young and the three eldest boys were possibly by this time too old to start. In a way it was an idyllic sort of time. The sun, at least in recollection, seemed to shine perpetually. I remember being chased in crazy excitement round and round a great clump of turf by one of the Daly children, Cissie I think was her name, and my first experience of human guile when she doubled back and confronted me as I came full tilt around a corner. There were explorations through the fields, and along the canal. Trivial activities stick in the mind, gathering wild strawberries, 'assisting' at the haymaking, swinging on gates. Fergus and I, and later Maeve, generally knocked about together, and likewise Gearóid, Ciarán and Brian formed a trio who were bent on more serious pursuits. Gearóid had a pair of enviable wooden stilts and these prompted a burst of invention whereby everybody began to move above the ground on empty tins which had contained Tate and Lyle's Golden Syrup. This form of stilt was controlled by a loop of string which was held in the hand. Other tins, Benger's food, Neave's food and polish tins were also useful raw material and the means whereby Gearóid in particular conducted experiments in steam compression. The tins were partly filled with water, sealed and subjected to heat, and there were frequent loud explosions. The rest of us learned something from these experiments, and amused ourselves in the same way, sometimes piercing the tin with a nail and watching the steam hissing out, until in exasperation the lid blew off.

We were all, at a certain age, perpetually frustrated by the lack of wheels and the difficulty of making them or devising a reasonable substitute—rollers or the like. Doubtless there is a deep human craving for wheeled transport, and ours was probably whetted by the thrill of propelling the high pram and being propelled in it. There was, indeed, a home-made four-wheeled cart which could be steered by the ubiquitous loop of string held in the hand, but its seating capacity was limited. The pram, with its unseen but often audible occupant, was usually in the background of whatever activity was afoot, and its large wheels were contemplated with envious eyes, but nobody had the courage to remove them. Being conveyed in farm carts with their peculiar bone-penetrating vibration is also one of the pleasures of recollection.

The most notable inventive activity associated with Tullamore was the showing of 'motion' pictures by Ciarán and Brian. The idea must have come from visits to cinema shows which were held in a hall in

Tullamore, but the method they devised was, I imagine, unique, and rightly so. They drew pictures on long strips of white paper. This 'film' was then made translucent by being soaked in paraffin oil and the pictures were passed through a species of home-made magic lantern. Surprisingly the oil had no clouding effect on line or colour or on the clarity of the printed words which issued from the mouths of the characters. The light power came from a paraffin wick-lamp and the danger of fire must have been great. After a day or two of intense activity on the part of the film-makers the rest of us were invited to see the pictures, being first requested to seek the admission money from our mother. She would give us whatever money she had handy but with no precise regard to the number going or the stated price of admission. It did not matter greatly. It was not a seller's market. The shows were held in a large shed that served as a garage, or in one of the commodious outhouses which ran along one side of the yard.

As far as I know Ciarán was the only member of the family who actually wrote stories in Tullamore. They had to be in book form and he used to buy notebooks for the purpose in a shop in Tullamore called McGorry's, which I am glad to say still thrives. Brian certainly composed stories but they were for the screen. For these screen stories both had invented and named a chief character with extraordinary powers and these characters were frequently in conflict with each other. Not only that, but we lesser lights, as yet illiterate, were sometimes threatened with a visitation from one or other of these formidable creations. In imitation we all, right through the family, created our own special character which took on a certain reality within our own immediate circle. Fergus once announced to me that his own creature, Breeshtchay Gavinn (the name is meaningless and not phonetically transcribable in English), was actually visiting the house, and, right enough, when we peered into the drawing-room we saw a confident stranger accompanied by two strange women conversing with our parents. Visitors were not very frequent in Tullamore but when they came it was a pleasant diversion. We got biscuits or even cake, and the visitors often obliged with money, a mysterious and chronically scarce commodity which we spent immediately if we could, or else lost.

We left Tullamore in 1923 and came to Dublin to Herbert Place, a long Georgian terrace flanking the banks of the Grand Canal whose higher reaches we had known in the heart of Offaly. One time in his column, 'Cruiskeen Lawn', Brian referred casually to The Beeches, Cappincur, and it must have startled the people who then lived there to find their house inexplicably publicized. Herbert Place and such environs as Wilton Place and the canal figure in *The Hard Life*, and for that matter, the stone stairs mentioned in a part of *At Swim-Two-Birds* are certainly the basement steps of 25 Herbert Place. At the time of his last illness some of us were talking about Tullamore and Brian said he had been thinking of making a visit there and elsewhere to renew old links. It was a visit never made in the flesh, but the going back of the mind which prompted it was the substance, the real place the shadow.

School and formal education became a reality for all of us in Dublin. Gearóid, Ciarán and Brian were sent to Synge St School while the rest of us who were of an age went to the nearby school at Haddington Road. We spoke Irish among ourselves and this, perhaps, along with our isolated upbringing, caused some friction at first with some of our school mates. At any rate, we had all to defend ourselves with our fists, which we did savagely and successfully. Ciarán records that at Synge Street Brian was an exception in this respect. He was able to deter by some personal quality, perhaps a piercing quality in his gaze, which rendered him immune from physical attack. At Synge Street the three boys were put into the fourth year and remained there for three years. The adjustment from a free and easy life to one in which time and activities were very largely controlled must have been painful. Ciarán says that they found themselves comparatively backward in mathematical subjects; in Irish and English they were in advance, were more widely read than others, mature and developed in their critical judgment. When we moved to Blackrock in 1927, five of us were sent to Blackrock College. Gearóid and Ciarán went into the sixth year and Brian into the fifth. We won practically all the prizes in our various classes the first year, a fact which established our studious reputation for years to come. In fact we were anything but studious. We did little or no 'homework', had literally no time for it. Now, after many years in education, I can only approve those early instincts. I can think of nothing more useless than many types of written 'exercises' unless it be to attempt to correct the same. What we did at home, apart from reading anything in sight, was to take things apart to see how they worked —with the result that they often ceased to work—to dismantle clocks, to unscrew anything that could be unscrewed, to attempt to construct steam engines and other mechanisms with inadequate knowledge and materials, so that nothing ever came to anything—all this may have been more destructive than writing exercises but educationally it was not inferior.

In Synge Street Brian took a particular interest in Physics and Chemistry, and developed (if that is the word) an interest in photography which he retained for many years. No doubt the period from 1923 to 1927, when the family lived in Herbert Place, when Brian attended school and passed from twelve to sixteen years, was a formative period; but there is nothing (at least that I am aware of) to indicate literary preoccupations. Fergus reminds me that in Herbert Place both Ciarán and Brian each wrote a 'newspaper'. Brian's was called *The Observer*. I do not know how long these continued, but Ciarán points out that the inspiration for this activity came from the visits of George Gormley who came fairly often to the house. The talk was often of the office and newspaper work. In any case, a great number of boys go through a period in which they write their own papers or magazines. Similar activities, the writing or making up of stories had gone on in Tullamore, where, apart from the books available at home, there was a local lending library. Both Ciarán and Brian were good at drawing and later all their school books were covered with extravagant and fantastic line drawings, mostly of human heads.

No. 25 Herbert Place is a large, five-storey house which defied even our large and growing family to occupy fully. The result was that the three spacious rooms on the top floor were left empty and unfurnished. This area was a godsend to us for all sorts of indoor activities. Fergus and I had a very extensive clockwork railway laid out in one room, Brian set up a darkroom in another for his photographic work.

Singing seems to me now to be an enviable accomplishment, and, from a musical point of view, there was a good tradition in our father's family. His own father was a music teacher. Our mother was a good singer, so was her brother, Eugene, and her brother, Joe, was not only a singer but a versatile musician. In our own family Ciarán played the piano and Brian studied the violin. Fergus had the gift of absolute pitch. But no male member of the family (except Michael), as far as I know, ever sang a song or even attempted to. Our uncle Joe did his level best with one after another, putting us through the scales, testing our voices, going over the words of suitable songs, accompanying on the piano, singing 'with us', but whenever he stopped singing himself, there was not a sound, nothing. Even the offer of money failed to elicit a note.

I cannot explain this reluctance. Even when visitors came and were asked for a song, many of us would have to steal from the room in case, if a high note occurred, we gave offence by an irresistible desire to laugh. Whenever the younger members of the family, Nessa, Nuala and Sheila, attempted to put on some show for the family, a 'concert', they were seized with uncontrollable laughter at the first bar and the whole thing ended in disaster. Even if the show was some sort of play, a dispute was heard behind the scenes as to who should go out first, and the grown-up and fed-up audience, having waited in vain, would leave in a body. Our parents and visiting relatives grew very wary of paying in advance for admission to any such diversions. All such things were fated, it seems to come to a sudden end if they ever even began. One day in Herbert Place Brian spent a long time making a cow's head out of a large brown-paper bag for some 'play'. It was a very realistic head when finished, and the muffled voice within lowed very passably. The family assembled and the cow's head suddenly appeared and bellowed loudly, whereupon Maeve, who was in the audience, became almost hysterical with fright and the show was immediately 'taken off'.

If anything worth while had been done in the way of home theatre, I am sure it would have met with an appreciative audience. It was because both our parents were so keen on theatre that they showed impatience at the lack of serious effort. They went, I suppose, to every play that appeared in Dublin, during our Herbert Place days, to every opera, to every performance by visiting companies, and were also regular filmgoers. Every theatre was within easy walking distance of the house, but even when we moved to Blackrock they continued to go in to theatres and shows very often. There was a very large accumulation of Abbey, Gate and Gaiety programmes in the house for a long time. I suppose they were all thrown out or burned eventually.

Our parents were thus out of the house on many evenings of the week and this led to an activity in their absence of a rather more sinister kind than home theatricals. The boys' bedroom was a large front room on the fourth floor. On dark nights, just as some passer-by or couple drew level with the house, Brian would touch off some 'flash-light' powder (which he had for his photography), which had been placed outside on the window-sill. There would be a blinding flash, which would have vanished before the party outside could know its location or what had caused it. The reaction of people and the remarks sometimes passed caused considerable amusement in the bedroom. For variety, as well as the flash, they began to throw stones into the roadway after passers-by were out of range. This naturally startled people even more. Some would hurry on, others might stop and try to discover what had happened. But all was again still and silent. If two or more had passed, some dialogue and speculation would usually follow.

When it was known that our parents were going out, Gearóid would ask Fergus and me to assemble suitable missiles for the night's work. Our parents never learned about this activity and it was discontinued abruptly when the boys saw or thought they saw policemen standing in the shadow of the trees which grew along the canal opposite the house. Someone no doubt had reported the strange occurrences.

It was a quiet and, at night, rather dark street, and one-sided, owing to the canal. There was nothing much on the far side of the canal except the back of MacEntaggart's Motor Works. By day there was not much traffic except on the canal where barges were continually passing. One day some men arranged a tug-of-war across the lock which adjoins the bridge leading into Percy Place. The front man on one side was pulled into the lock but was happily fished out in time as, apparently, he could not swim and was rather jarred.

In 1925 our father was appointed a Revenue Commissioner and in 1927 we moved to Blackrock, the last house-move for the family as a whole. We were sent to Blackrock College, where Brian spent two years before going to University College, Dublin. Blackrock College was and is famous for its devotion to rugby, but none of us showed any interest in the game except Gearóid. Brian told the senior mathematics teacher, Hugh Holohan, that rugby players should be taken behind the stand at Lansdowne Road and shot.

The next ten years is a period I cannot adequately describe. This is unfortunate insofar as literary critics may be concerned to discover matters in this chronicle of significance for the future author. As I reflect on what I have so far written, I see a catalogue of trivial and somewhat odd events and much that is commonplace. Brian's first strong urge to write becomes evident at University College, where he enlivened the students' magazine, *Comhthrom Féinne*, wrote much for it, not only in English but in Irish also, including archaic and humorous parodies of medieval language and style. There was much that was new and fresh in his contributions, for instance, not only the idea of writing medieval Irish but the acknowledgment in introductory remarks of the valuable work done by 'other scholars' like Dr Bergin (the distinguished Professor of Old Irish who taught in the College at the time). His humour was original and many-sided, his command of language formidable and there was an assurance and maturity in what he wrote that is not easily matched among undergraduates. He does not seem to have served his time as a writer but to have assumed magisterial status with a confidence which defied question. Books like *Die Harzreise*, which he was studying as texts prescribed for College courses, had already become the raw material for use in future novels. The more he became engrossed in writing the more he seemed able to do. In a short five- or six-year period he wrote not only *At Swim* and *The Third Policeman* but also the Irish satire, *An Béal Bocht* as well as a play, *Faustus Kelly*, helped to found and edited a humorous magazine, *Blather*, wrote for the *Bell* and other magazines, undertook a humorous column in the *Irish Times*. He abandoned one of his College pseudonyms, Brother Barnabas, and finally organized his work, according to its nature, under three pen-names, Flann O'Brien, Brian (O) Nolan and Myles na Gopaleen. (The first article of his *Irish Times* column was a sort of warning shot across the bows of unsuspecting readers and it sank without trace. It was signed An Broc (or The Badger). A week elapsed and in the next and subsequent articles the pseudonym was Myles na gCopaleen. Five articles appeared before readers began to write letters of protest or approval to the Editor.)

Life at University College brought new horizons. At home the inner family life was changing rapidly, at any rate for the eldest trio with whom this narrative is essentially concerned. Blackrock had brought new acquaintances, new friends. They were much with the Kenny boys, Joe and Desmond, who also went to Blackrock College and whose family lived near ours. Other families they became closely associated with were the Duffys and the McManus family. Dick McManus was a very close friend of Brian, and the selection from 'Cruiskeen Lawn' is dedicated to him. *The three were drawn much more to outside activities and influences, and acted much less in concert. Ciarán and Brian continued to share many pursuits but these were extraneous to the family.

Some of the old patterns persisted. Our father was a keen chess player and belonged to several clubs. We also joined and all shared in many strange encounters. Here too the new patterns mingled with the old, for Oscar Quigley was a noted chess player and also a boon companion in other more boisterous activities. But perhaps I should here call a halt in case I add pointlessly to an already extended narrative.

Our father died suddenly in 1937. Brian asked for his pen, a very old Waterman which he had used all his life. The hand changed but the

---

* The 'Cruiskeen Lawn' here referred to was a selection made from the early *Irish Times* pieces by Brian, and published in book form by Cahill & Co., Dublin.

pen wrote on. Family life too went on, but the road ahead was darkened by the shadow of grimmer times.

One or two trifles I may add. My mother sometimes recalled incidents concerning different members of the family. About Brian I remember two things she said. Once she observed him in infancy in his cot from a hidden vantage point. Thinking he was alone, he made great and urgent efforts and managed to get out of the cot, whereupon he crawled off at lightning speed towards the door. If this signifies a precocious curiosity, so be it. Later on, but while he was still hardly of an age to speak, she said that a charwoman who used to come to the house complained that the toddler had confronted her outside and asked: 'who gave you the allow to come up our path?' If that be claimed as betokening an early command of language, so be it.

He was always fond of puzzles and dined out on match tricks. Once Nessa, Brian and his wife, Evelyn, were out motoring, and in the evening arrived at some pub in the country which turned out to be chock-full of customers, all talking. The din was something fierce. Brian shouted to the two women not to worry, that he would have 'all these chiners quiet in two minutes'. He produced his favourite match puzzle, challenged anybody to solve it, and Nessa alleges that in no time at all all tongues were silent, all eyes bent on a pattern of matches which adorned every table.

Our mother died in 1956. I remember Brian asking helplessly how we ——s deserved or came to have the mother we had. There was no answer. He thought for a long time of writing something about her but it baffled him. Some things are beyond words.

NIALL SHERIDAN

Brian, Flann and Myles

(The Springtime of Genius)

When I first came to University College, Dublin, in the autumn of 1930, it had a student population of around 3,000. The main Faculties were housed in the heavy, grey building on Earlsfort Terrace, where the crucial debate on the Anglo-Irish Treaty had taken place eight years before. The scars left by the Civil War which followed the Treaty were still raw, and the new generation of students—or those of them who thought about these matters—were equally concerned about the cultural identity of the new State and its place in the wider intellectual context of Europe.

Dublin in those days still retained much of its faded Georgian elegance, and the social climate was informal, relaxed and tolerant—in spite of the economic depression and the residue of political bitterness left over from the Twenties. The mellow eighteenth-century façades had not yet been replaced by high-rise office blocks, the electric trams clattered noisily along the streets and droves of cyclists wove a carefree course through the traffic. The tradition of domestic entertaining was still strong, and there was no night in the week when some notable house was not open to a lively group of talkers, writers, artists and wits.

It might be George Russell's home in Rathgar, or Yeats in Rathfarnham, or Sarah Purser in Mespil Road, or Jimmy Montgomery— that wittiest and most urbane of Dubliners—on Merrion Road. The various social circles intersected and overlapped and conversation was

4. Brian O'Nolan as a boy

5. Brian O'Nolan in later years

6. Sandymount Strand, Dublin, Bloomsday, 1954. *Left to right*: John Ryan, Anthony Cronin, Brian O'Nolan, Patrick

still respected as an art. Everyone knew everyone else. Dublin was then the largest, and certainly the liveliest, village in the world.

During the early Thirties, University College attracted a remarkable group of students, whose various talents and interests reflected the political and intellectual climate of the time.

A leading member of that group was Denis Devlin (afterwards Irish Ambassador to Italy), who had already published—in collaboration with his friend Brian Coffey—a small collection of poems. A scholar in both Irish and French, he translated many of the French symbolist poets into Gaelic, and encouraged all of us to look towards Paris rather than London as our intellectual Mecca. He was at once gay, erudite and courteous. Devlin's thought was elegant and oblique, and he distilled into his poetry a remarkable fusion of learning, wit and lyric passion.

A close friend also was Donagh MacDonagh, son of Thomas MacDonagh, the executed 1916 leader. Don was an energetic, forthright person and a born organizer, who wrote with great fluency. His usual form of greeting was to pull a sheaf of new poems from his pocket and test them out on his friends. When we published together our first book (*Twenty Poems*), it was he who decided that we should settle the order of our names on the title-page by tossing a coin. I won the toss, but the modest success of the venture was mainly due to Donagh, who ruthlessly blackmailed friends and acquaintances into buying copies.

Another friend of ours, and a very memorable personality, was Charlie Donnelly, who began as a really promising poet and became by the age of twenty-two—when he was killed in the Spanish Civil War—a brilliant political theorist and, of all things, an acknowledged expert on military strategy. Small and frail-looking in physique, he was a person of astonishing moral and physical courage.

In the political and philosophical areas which interested him, Donnelly, for his age, had the most mature mind I have ever encountered. On his frequent visits to MacDonagh and myself (we lodged with a delightful Jewish family in Rathmines), he would often leave coyly behind him a selection of Marxist literature, in the hope that we might become converted. But we were both fundamentally apolitical and he eventually gave up his proselytising effort in wry despair.

He felt the outbreak of the Spanish Civil War to be a turning point in contemporary history, and when he told us that he intended to enlist and fight against Franco, we were saddened but not surprised. MacDonagh and I argued vehemently with him, pointing out that any fool could carry a rifle while he could do far more influential work by staying alive. There are echoes of that argument in the fine poem which MacDonagh wrote shortly after we got news of Charlie's death:

> Of what a quality is courage made
> That he who gently walked our city streets
> Talking of poetry, philosophy,
> Spinoza, Keats,
> Should lie like any martyred soldier,
> His brave and fertile brain dried quite away
> And the limbs that carried him from cradle
>   to death's outpost
> Growing down into a foreign clay.

Other contemporaries and friends were Cyril Cusack and Liam Redmond, who were later to make international reputations in the theatre and in films. Cusack, at that time, was more interested in writing than in acting, but the strength of his hereditary theatrical tradition eventually won out. Redmond did some remarkable work in the Dramatic Society, and I remember particularly his production of *Murder in the Cathedral*, for which Eliot himself came across to Dublin. Another notable personality was Niall Montgomery, whose quick wit was sometimes so elliptical and recondite that he seemed to be telling jokes to himself.

But the most striking talent among that variously gifted generation of students was undoubtedly Brian Nolan, whom I first met early in 1931 in the Main Hall of University College. I have a vivid memory of that shortish figure, with a round, sallow face, hair already thinning and small but prominent front teeth: the incarnation of a Satanic cherub. Except for his alert and piercing gaze, he might have seemed, to the casual observer, a rather ordinary person. He was very far from that.

Brian had already begun to achieve a certain notoriety and was a regular contributor to the College Magazine, which had been rejuvenated (under the title *Comhthrom Féinne*) in May 1931. He frequently used the Irish form of his name, Brian Ua Nualláin, but he had also started to create a new literary personality under the pseudonym of 'Brother Barnabas'.

(The group of students I have mentioned, together with some kindred spirits, formed in those years a sort of intellectual Mafia, which strongly influenced the cultural and social life of University College, and controlled—through some rather dubious electoral ruses—most of the College Clubs and Societies concerned with the Arts. The editorship of the magazine was usually passed from one member of the group to another. It was a useful mouthpiece, and entitled us to tickets for the theatres and cinemas, and also review copies of books, which could be resold for half the published price.)

Brian's creative power was already apparent in his elaboration of fantastic situations. 'Brother Barnabas' soon became a figure of legendary proportions—statesman, diplomat, international financier, the Grey Eminence behind countless plots and strategems. When I took over the magazine, we worked hand-in-glove and *Comhthrom Féinne* became a weird mixture of poetry, parody, literary criticism and mock-sensationalism.

We usually reserved the centre-spread for some new and startling revelation from Brother Barnabas, introduced by screaming headlines:

RUMOURED CLOSING OF EARLSFORT TERRACE
FISTICUFFS AT BADEN-BADEN
Politicus Hits Out

×   ×   ×
BROTHER BARNABAS THRASHED
Extraordinary Scenes
×   ×   ×

35

LIONEL PRUNE MUST GO, SAYS B.B.
'A Journeyman Dilettante'
SCATHING ATTACK

His exuberant fantasy was usually seasoned with the sharp tang of reality. I recall another invention:

GRADUATE CUT TO PIECES BY EXPRESS TRAIN
Brilliant New Insurance Scheme
Free Gifts For Readers

The scheme referred to was elaborated in minute and gruesome detail, and a panel on the same page carried this announcement:

'THIS WEEK'S PRIZE' OF FIVE SHILLINGS
For the Most Interesting Claim
Awarded to Mr. P. Reilly (Ballyjamesduff)
(*Two feet severed at ankles—Moving-machine mishap at harvesting*

Brian was continually bubbling over with intellectual energy and high spirits, but there was already more to this than the usual undergraduate exhibitionism. Most of us, I think, recognized that he possessed something more profound and disturbing than mere talent. Behind that penetrating gaze lay the *saeva indignatio* of a Swift and he was rapidly achieving the capacity to give it devastating expression.

Indeed, his command of his medium was already almost total. Looking back, it seems to me that he burst on the scene fully equipped as a writer. One is reminded of his own creation, John Furriskey in *At Swim-Two-Birds*, who was born with a full set of teeth, a flourishing head of black hair, and possessing 'an unusually firm grasp of the Latin idiom and a knowledge of Physics extending from Boyle's Law to the Leclanche Cell and the Greasepot Photometer'.

At one stage, while I was running the magazine, Brian (to his great delight) landed me into an absurd predicament with the College Authorities.

I asked him to write a series of short fiction pieces dealing with contemporary life, a sort of Dublin *Decameron*. He undertook to do this, but only on condition that he be allowed to write in Old Irish. I agreed to this, and he then explained that he would be addressing an audience of only three, presumably that celebrated trio of scholars, Osborn Bergin, D. A. Binchy and Richard Best. Because of this deliberate limitation of readership, he argued, there could be no question of any form of editorial censorship. This seemed reasonably valid to me and we went ahead.

There were ominous rumblings soon after the first instalment appeared. Brian had apparently outdone Rabelais and the Three Wise Men, greatly tickled by the bawdy humour, could not resist retelling the choicest episodes to some of their colleagues. A good story, like bad news, travels fast and I soon found myself summoned before the then President of the College, Dr Denis Coffey, on the rather unusual charge of publishing obscene matter, written in Old Irish, in the semi-official University organ.

Dr Coffey was himself a notable scholar and a courteous gentleman, who looked like some fashionable musicologist of the Edwardian era. His favourite form of transport was a horse-drawn cab (he was allergic to the internal combustion engine), he wore a high collar and was reputed never to have used a fountain pen. But for all his surface conservatism, he understood the younger generation and was an excellent President.

Before the crucial interview, there were consultations with our legal advisers (the place was stiff with briefless barristers) and I was advised that the best line of defence was a simple plea of criminal negligence. I followed this line, admitting at once that I had published material which I could not read or evaluate. This proved a fortunate gambit, since Dr Coffey confessed to a similar degree of cultural deprivation. He, too, was completely ignorant of Old Irish.

Mutual regret over our cultural shortcomings generated a more congenial atmosphere, and we moved on to general topics, including a consideration of the ethical and metaphysical aspects of the Hippocratic Oath and a lengthy (if somewhat one-sided) discussion of the iconography of St Patrick in Scandinavia—topics not frequently canvassed among my student cronies.

Taking the ball on the hop, I introduced a more mundane note and reminded Dr Coffey that the College Chess Club had fallen into abeyance. It was surely regrettable that a game so closely associated with the legendary heroes of ancient Ireland should be utterly neglected in our National University. The President agreed heartily and allowed me a grant of £25 towards re-establishing the Chess Club. We parted on excellent terms. In those Hungry Thirties one could have a lot of fun with that kind of money.

Brian and I were among the very few regular chess players then in the College. As there was no existing committee, I appointed him President of the Club, reserving to myself the less gaudy—but more significant—office of Treasurer.

His style of playing chess was very characteristic and became part of the image he liked to project to the outside world. He would sit glowering at the board, lips drawn back from his rabbit-like teeth, making odd hissing sounds as he drew in his breath in concentration. Suddenly, he would seize a piece and plonk it down in its new position, making every move with an air of delivering the *coup-de-grace*. This combination of play-acting and moral blackmail had a paralysing effect on simpler souls and gave him a reputation quite out of proportion to his skill at the game.

At one stage, he developed an attacking combination which he called the 'Nolan Phalanx' and would astonish his more naïve fellow students with accounts of the famous victories this had brought him. Alekhine had retired to Russia, a broken man, after an epic match in Vienna, and he had polished off Capablanca in twenty-seven moves when they met at Katmandu, of all likely places.

But the weapon which had wrought such devastation among the masters did not guarantee invincibility against humbler rivals, and I recall him spitting with fury when a red-haired student from the wilds of Co. Cavan unhorsed him with a home-made variation of the Ruy Lopez gambit, which he had elaborated during the long nights after Samhain.

He greatly enjoyed creating legendary adventures for himself. In some previous incarnation, he had escaped from Russia on a six-horse sleigh, during a blizzard, escorting the daughter of a Grand Duke with three million pounds worth of jewels sewn in her clothing, while a horde of starving wolf-packs howled at their heels. So well established did this myth become that, years later, it surfaced in a biographical note on Brian in *Time* magazine.

In the summer of 1934 he found a new outlet for his energy when he started a comic magazine, with financial backing from some friends in the publishing and advertising world. The magazine—*Blather*, subtitled 'the Voice from the Back of the Hall'—had a short but hilarious career. Brian edited the paper and wrote the vast bulk of the material. His Byzantine love of ingenuity and complexity was expressed in a series of crazy competitions, conundrums, riddles and parodies. This was the first public flowering of that element of fantasy which blossomed so gaily in the 'Myles na gCopaleen' column and so ominously in the world of *The Third Policeman*

His preoccupation with the legendary and the apocryphal once again found an outlet in his creation of The O'Blather (statesman, sportsman, scholar, philosopher, etc., etc.) and his idiot son, Blazes O'Blather. The O'Blather was the successor of Brother Barnabas and the precursor of Sir Myles na gCopaleen.

The impending collapse of *Blather* in January 1935 was signalled by a characteristic headline:

OUR TOTTERING CIRCULATION
Are we Too Good to Last?

Like the rest of us, Brian read everything he could get his hands on. Eliot was a big influence with us, as were the French writers *The Waste Land* had brought back into vogue. We felt that the Anglo-Irish Renaissance was already a spent force, though the stature of Yeats— especially since *The Tower* poems—was beyond question. Sam Beckett, whom we knew personally, had opened new horizons with *Murphy*. Joyce, of course, was in the very air we breathed.

Of the Americans, we were reading Hergesheimer, Cabell, Dos Passos, Hemingway, and Scott Fitzgerald. The nineteenth-century Russians were required reading, and there was also a lively interest in Proust, Kafka and Kierkegaard. Brian greatly admired these last three writers, but this would not prevent him, in a sudden chauvinistic pose, from thundering against 'layabouts from the slums of Europe poking around in their sickly little psyches'.

We were constantly preoccupied with literary theories and with more mundane schemes designed to raise ready cash, a very scarce commodity in those days. Brian proclaimed that the principles of the Industrial Revolution must be applied to literature. The time had come when books should be made, not written—and a 'made' book had a better chance of becoming a best-seller.

If one thousand monkeys were chained to one thousand typewriters for a month, they would undoubtedly produce a steady stream of best-sellers and, probably, a few masterpieces. After further consideration, he announced that he had abandoned this project on purely economic grounds. What would be the cost of maintaining a thousand adult monkeys in good writing condition for a month? Where would we house his simian authors? Then there was the cost of hiring typewriters and purchasing several tons of flea powder.

His interest soon shifted to a suggestion of mine—the All-Purpose Opening Speech. This was to be one endless sentence, grammatically correct, and so devoid of meaning that it could be used on any conceivable occasion: inaugurating a President, consecrating a Cathedral, laying a foundation-stone, presenting an inscribed watch to a long-serving employee. This notion delighted him, and he decided that it must be given to the world, translated into every known language. If nation could speak fluently to nation, without any risk of communicating anything, international tension would decline. The Speech would be a major contribution to civilization, enabling any inarticulate lout who might lever himself into power to emerge (after a brief rehearsal) as a new Demosthenes.

I was to make the original draft in English. Denis Devlin was to undertake the translation into French and Brian himself would do the Irish and German versions.

I can remember only the opening portions of the Speech, which ran (still incomplete) to some 850 words:

Unaccustomed as I am to public speaking, and reluctant as I am to parade my inability before such a critical and distinguished gathering, comprising—need I say—all that is best in the social, political, and intellectual life of our country, a country, may I add, which has played no inconsiderable part in the furtherance of learning and culture, not to speak of religion, throughout all the lands of the known globe, where, although the principles inculcated in that learning and that culture have now become temporarily obfuscated in the pursuit of values as meretricious in seeming as they must prove inadequate in realisation, nevertheless, having regard to the ethical and moral implications of the contemporary situation, etc, etc, etc.

When the translations had been completed we had a reading in Devlin's home. Any rubbish can be made to sound impressive in French, and Denis had produced a superb version, rhythmic, mellifluous and authoritative. It conveyed (to our delight and amazement) even less meaning than the original.

Brian (who delighted in the simplest sleight-of-hand), whipped a walrus moustache from his pocket, fixed it under his nose and read his Irish version, in a wickedly accurate impersonation of our Professor of Irish, Dr Douglas Hyde, later the first President of Ireland.

'What do you think of that?' he asked, looking from one to the other.

Denis told him that he admired his *brio* but deplored his occasional slurring of consonants. I told him that listening to his delivery was like wading through warm stirabout in one's bare feet.

Undeterred by this mixed reception, Brian quickly replaced the walrus moustache with a toothbrush affair and poured out his German translation in imitation of Hitler at a Nuremburg Rally. As he ground out the Teutonic gutturals, spitting and snarling in comic menace, he knew he had made the hit of the evening.

The most ambitious of all Brian's literary schemes for making money was probably quite feasible, though a little ahead of its time. He called us together in the 'snug' of Grogan's pub in Leeson Street to announce that nobody had yet produced the Great Irish Novel. The time had come when it must be written or, rather, manufactured.

This great saga (working title: *Children of Destiny*) would deal with

41

the fortunes of an Irish family over a period of almost a century, starting in 1840. It would illuminate a whole panorama of social and political history—the Famine Years, faction fights, evictions, lecherous landlords and modest maidens, emigration, the horrors of the coffin ships, etc., etc.

In America, a member of the family would rise through ward politics and Tammany Hall to the political heights, returning to Ireland to fight in the 1916 Rising, and dying gallantly (in full public view)—the last man to leave the burning ruins of the General Post Office. His son, graduating from politics to high finance, would become the first Irish-American Catholic President of the United States.

Brian proposed that he, Devlin, MacDonagh and I should write the book in sections and then stick the pieces together in committee. At least, we'd come cheaper than those monkeys.

A vast market was ready and waiting. Compulsory education had produced millions of semi-literates, who were partial to 'a good read'. So it must be a big book, weighing at least two-and-a-half pounds. We must give them length without depth, splendour without style. Existing works would be plundered wholesale for material, and the ingredients of the saga would be mainly violence, patriotism, sex, religion, politics and the pursuit of money and power.

Children of Destiny would be the precursor of a new literary movement, the first masterpiece of the Ready-Made or Reach-Me-Down School. There would be continuous action, a series of thrilling climaxes and great set-pieces and crowd scenes. In its power and scope, it would make the surge and thunder of the Odyssey seem like the belching and gurgling of a baby in swaddling clothes.

He himself would write the religious segment. This revolved around a scion of the family who (surviving a breach-of-promise action by a farmer's daughter) pursued his vocation with such dedication and cunning that he eventually broke the Italian stranglehold on the Papacy, to become Pope Patrick I.

While the Papal election is in progress, an immense throng (including a strong Irish contingent) fills St Peter's Square, tensely awaiting the plume of rising smoke which will indicate the result of the voting.

Here, Brian had invented a very characteristic touch—an Irish Monsignor, in charge of the smoke-signals, smuggles in two sods of turf and, as the white smoke rises above the Sistine Chapel, the unmistakable tang of the bog, wafting out over the Bernini colonnades, tells his waiting countrymen that a decision (and the right one) has been reached.

For Pope Patrick I, Brian had planned a splendid apotheosis, which would bring the great work to its close. At the age of eighty-seven, he travels to his native land to perform the ceremony of throwing in the ball at the start of an All-Ireland Football Final between Cavan and Kildare, as the Tricolour and the Papal Flag (now incorporating a green harp) flutter proudly over Croke Park.

The description of the game would be couched in the florid sporting jargon so beloved of Irish provincial sportswriters:

'In the closing minutes of the opening moiety, the Short Grass man —a tower of strength in attack as in defence—drove in a daisy-cutter which rattled the twines, to the consternation of the baffled Breffni custodian . . .'

It's a ding-dong struggle and, with thirty seconds of play remaining, Cavan (leading by one point) appears to have the title in the bag. Suddenly, breaking clear of a mêlée, the redoubtable Short Grass man —'a veritable Scarlet Pimpernel at midfield'—sends a high, dropping ball across the bar from forty yards out for the equalizing point. A DRAW! The vast crowd comes to its feet in a frenzy of excitement.

But the tension has been too much for the aged Pontiff. Stricken by a sudden seizure, he sinks back dying, literally, in the arms of his countrymen, while the sun descends flamboyantly behind the Railway goal and 'Faith of our Fathers' thunders into the evening sky from eighty thousand Irish throats.

All this—and Heaven, too! Brian glared around him in triumph, as if challenging us to dissent. What more could any reader (or, indeed, any Pope) ask for at seven-and-sixpence a copy?

Work began at once on the great scheme. Brian ransacked *Hadrian VII* for ecclesiastical background material and Vatican colour stuff. MacDonagh discovered a history student who was doing a thesis on the Famine. Devlin bent his mind to the French scene, since one of the characters was to follow the trail of the Wild Geese and become, like the Hennessys, Garveys, O'Donnells and Lynchs, a world-renowned figure in the wine trade. My contribution, at that stage, was to write an account of the Football Final and also of the Grand National. It had been arranged that another member of this remarkable family was to win the famous Steeplechase against unbelievable odds.

There was a short period of hectic activity, but the Great Irish Novel never materialized.

One morning Brian told me that he had started to write a book on his own. The plot, he explained, was simple: it would concern an author, Dermot Trellis, who was writing a book about certain characters who, in turn, were revenging themselves by writing about him.

'That's not a plot,' I told him. 'It's a conspiracy.'

The characters, he went on, would be drawn from legend, history, imagination and the works of past writers. Conventional notions of Time would be scorned. Past, present and future would be abolished, and the work would exist in a supra-Bergsonian continuum—communicating simultaneously on several planes of consciousness and also on various subliminal levels.

He could write quickly when a theme absorbed him and soon he began to show me sections of the book as it progressed, explaining the *rationale* behind each episode and its place in the overall design. Very soon, these sessions began to form part of the text, and I found myself (under the name Brinsley) living a sort of double life at the autobiographical core of a work which was in the process of creation.

In *At Swim-Two-Birds* he recreates the mood and atmosphere of our discussions with astonishing fidelity and an uncanny ear for the rhythms of ordinary speech:

'A friend of mine, Brinsley, came in and looked about him at the door. He came forward at my invitation and asked me to give him a cigarette. I took out my "butt" and showed it to him in the hollow of my hand.

That is all I have, I said, affecting a pathos in my voice.

By God you're the queer bloody man, he said. Are you sitting on a newspaper?

I was talking to a friend of yours last night, I said drily. I mean Mr Trellis. He has bought a ream of ruled foolscap and is starting on his story. He is compelling all his characters to live with him in the Red Swan Hotel so that he can keep an eye on them and see that there is no boozing.

I see, said Brinsley.

Most of them are characters used in other books, chiefly the works of another great writer called Tracy. There is a cowboy in Room 13 and Mr McCool, a hero of old Ireland, is on the floor above. The cellar is full of leprechauns.

What are they all going to do? asked Brinsley.

Nature of his tone: Without intent, tired, formal.

Trellis, I answered steadily, is writing a book on sin and the wages attaching thereto. He is a philosopher and a moralist. He is appalled by the spate of sexual and other crimes recorded in recent times in the newspapers—particularly in those published on Saturday night.

Nobody will read the like of that, said Brinsley.'

As the book progressed, Brian gleefully borrowed any material that came to hand. One day, I showed him a sales letter from a Newmarket tipster and it turned up *in toto* in the next wad of typescript that he produced. About the same time, I had done some translations from Catullus and he asked me for a copy of one of these. Later, it came out like this in *At Swim*:

'That same afternoon I was sitting on a stool in an intoxicated condition in Grogan's licensed premises. Adjacent stools bore the forms of Brinsley and Kelly, my two true friends. The three of us were occupied in putting glasses of stout into the interior of our bodies and expressing by fine disputation the resulting sense of physical and mental well-being. . . .

Do not let us forget that I have to buy *Die Harzreise*.

Do not let us forget that.

Harzreise, said Brinsley. There is a house in Dalkey called Heart-rise.

Brinsley then put his dark chin on the cup of a palm and leaned

45

in thought on the counter, overlooking his drink, gazing beyond the frontier of the world.

What about another jar? said Kelly.

Ah, Lesbia, said Brinsley. The finest thing I ever wrote. How many kisses, Lesbia, you ask, would serve to sate this hungry love of mine?—As many as the Libyan sands that bask along Cyrene's shore where pine-trees wave, where burning Jupiter's untended shrine lies near to old King Battus' sacred grave:

Three stouts, called Kelly.

Let them be endless as the stars at night, that stare upon the lovers in a ditch—so often would love-crazed Catullus bite your burning lips, that prying eyes should not have power to count, nor evil tongues bewitch, the frenzied kisses that you gave and got.

Before we die of thirst, called Kelly, will you bring us *three more stouts*. God, he said to me, it's in the desert you'd think we were.

That's good stuff, you know, I said to Brinsley.

A picture came before my mind of the lovers at their hedge-pleasure in the pale starlight, no sound from them, his fierce mouth burying into hers.

Bloody good stuff, I said.

Kelly, invisible to my left, made a slapping noise.

The best I ever drank, he said.'

The scene in the house of Michael Byrne, 'painter, poet, composer, pianist, master-printer, tactician, an authority on ballistics', recalls that remarkable man, Cecil ffrench Salkeld. At this period, it was Cecil's habit to rise about six in the evening and spend the entire night in reading, talk or the development of his many artistic projects:

'You're a terrible man for the blankets, said Kerrigan.

I'm not ashamed to admit that I love my bed, said Byrne. She was my first friend, my foster-mother, my dearest comforter . . .

He paused and drank.

Her warmth, he continued, kept me alive when my mother bore me. She still nurtures me, yielding without stint the parturition of her cosy womb. She will nurse me gently in my last hour and faithfully hold my cold body when I am dead. She will look bereaved when I am gone.

This speech did not please us, bringing to each of us our last personal end. We tittered in cynical fashion.

Glass tinkle at his teeth notified a sad concluding drink.

Brinsley gave a loud question.

Wasn't Trellis another great bed-bug?

He was, I answered.

I'm afraid I never heard of Trellis, said Byrne. Who is Trellis?

A member of the author class, I said.

Did he write a book on Tactics? I fancy I met him in Berlin. A tall man with glasses.

He has been in bed for the last twenty years, I said.

You are writing a novel of course? said Byrne.

He is, said Brinsley, and the plot has him well in hand.'

I remember that last remark of mine very clearly, and it gives one a curious *frisson* to find the whole scene and mood preserved with such a fusion of factual accuracy and imaginative truth.

When I got through the final draft of the book (there must have been over 800 pages of typescript), I told him it was too long. He had got such fun out of sending-up the Fenian cycle that he over-indulged himself and the weight of this material seriously unbalanced the latter half of the book.

Like any writer with a big task just completed, Brian had no wish to return to it. Besides, he was already taken up with planning another novel.

'I am sick of the sight of it,' he told me. 'What about cutting it yourself?'

I took out about one-fifth of the text before the book went to Longmans, who published it on the strong recommendation of Graham Greene. Before the publication date, Brian gave me one of his six complimentary copies in which he had written:

Sheraton
To Mr Sheridan I unload
This celestial commode—
Of that particular accessory
It can be said that it is necessary.

About a month later (May 1939), he acted as best man at my wedding. We were honeymooning in Paris, and I had told him that I would be seeing James Joyce. At the foot of the gangway, as we boarded the boat at Dun Laoghaire, he handed me a copy of the book and asked me to bring it to Joyce (I hadn't seen it around during the ceremony or at the hurried breakfast afterwards). On the fly-leaf he had written the dedication:

'To James Joyce from the author,
Brian O'Nolan, with plenty of
what's on page 305'

On that page Brian had underlined the phrase '*diffidence of the author*'.

Joyce was then in the process of moving into a new flat at 34 rue des Vignes, which was to be his last home in Paris. He was alone in the flat when I called, and he said Sam Beckett had already praised *At Swim-Two-Birds* very highly to him and that he looked forward to reading it.

His sight was so precarious that he had long given up reading fiction; indeed, he rarely showed any interest in contemporary writers, apart from his great admiration for Yeats and Eliot and his friendship with Sam Beckett, Padraic Colum and James Stephens—born on the same day as himself, a significant coincidence for Joyce.

We spent most of the afternoon in his sunny living-room, as yet only partly furnished with two armchairs, a coffee-table on which lay a copy of *Finnegans Wake* and a large woven rug on the wooden floor. It had been given to him, he told me, by an admirer of *Finnegans Wake* and the design illustrated the course of the River Liffey from its source to its mouth. A few pictures hung on the walls, including the famous Tuohy portrait of his father, John Stanislaus.

48

Joyce greatly enjoyed *At Swim-Two-Birds*, which he considered a comic work of remarkable creative power. (He often complained that too many of the serious commentators on *Ulysses* failed to recognize that it was essentially 'a funny book'.) Although the War was less than three months away, he made every effort to have Brian's book brought to the notice of the most influential French critics. When he had left Paris for the South, and shortly before his last journey to Switzerland, he was still writing to me on this subject.

At Swim-Two-Birds was, I am certain, the last novel he read. Ten years later, in a catalogue of the small library left behind in his Paris flat, Brian's presentation copy is listed and described as: *Livre très aimé de Joyce.*

Some time in the autumn of that year, or early in 1940, Brian started a bogus literary controversy in the correspondence columns of the *Irish Times*—a prank that was to change his career and bring him a new dimension of fame, under a new pseudonym.

Writing under several different names, he proceeded to carry on furious arguments on many topics, satirizing *en passant* almost every established literary figure. Before long, many notable personalities joined the mêlée and the whole affair exploded into a giant display of fireworks, a mixture of satire, polemics, criticism, savage invective and sheer nonsense. This running controversy (encouraged by the Editor) eventually filled a large space in the paper and gave a substantial boost to the circulation.

A fine peak of absurdity was reached when Brian—writing under the name 'Hazel Ellis'—aimed a devastating broadside at Micheál MacLiammóir and Hilton Edwards of the Gate Theatre. As it happened, there *was* a real Hazel Ellis, who had (to make matters worse) recently had a play successfully produced at the Gate. She immediately rushed into print with a disclaiming letter, proclaiming herself a fervent admirer of Micheál and Hilton. Brian took this turn of events in his stride and immediately replied—again under the name 'Hazel Ellis'— denouncing this lady as an obvious imposter.

By this time the Editor, R. M. Smyllie (though enjoying the fun), began to feel that things were getting out of hand. The word 'libel' was being whispered around the office. One afternoon his gruff voice came across the phone to me:

'I hear you are a pal of this fellow. I want to meet him right away. Bring him along this evening.'

'Which of them?', I asked.

Smyllie gave an angry growl: 'Get the bugger along here and none of your bloody nonsense,' and slammed down the phone.

Smyllie was a pretty distinctive figure on the Dublin scene at that time. Appointed Editor in 1934, he had brought a new liveliness and breadth to the *Irish Times*. In this managerial era, it is hardly possible to distinguish an Editor from a Chief Accountant, but in Smyllie's case there was no problem of identity. His huge bulk was topped by a massive head under a very wide hat and his normal gear (perhaps a brown sports-jacket, green corduroy trousers, puce pullover, red socks and brown boots) made a striking ensemble.

His arrival at the *Irish Times* office in the late afternoon could be something of an event. In anticipation of his coming, the front office was frequently occupied by a straggle of suppliants—impoverished old acquaintances to whom he gave small sums of money, crackpots seeking publicity for their crazy schemes, a well-known briefless barrister needing money for a cocaine 'fix', an elderly lady from some respectable suburb, banging her umbrella on the counter and demanding an interview with the Editor.

Like many heavy men, Smyllie was surprisingly nimble on his feet and could move swiftly through the beseeching throng and up the stairs to the next floor. Sometimes, if too sorely tried, he might turn on the landing with a sweeping gesture and quell the mob with a shout:

'Pissmires and warlocks, stand aside!'

Then he would vanish into his den, leaving trailing clouds of pipe smoke in his wake.

There would be a brief Editorial Conference, after which he would adjourn to the Palace Bar, in Fleet Street, to hold court among his cronies.

We went along there and found the Editor seated at a corner table, wearing his wide hat and a pair of black knitted gloves. A large Scotch stood in front of him. (I once asked him about his curious habit of drinking with his gloves on, and he explained it by telling me that he had promised his Mother never to touch liquor). Smyllie was intrigued by Brian from the start. He was well accustomed to dealing with intelligent people and had gathered a very bright group of young men around him on the *Irish Times*, but this was something quite outside his previous experience. They hit it off from the beginning.

Smyllie had a wonderful editorial flair, an unerring nose for talent, and before many Scotches had vanished, he had engaged Brian to write a regular column for the paper. At first he wrote in Irish only, then bilingually, and later almost entirely in English. It was the beginning of a commitment to journalism which was to last for twenty-five years, until shortly before his death. The column, written under the pseudonym of 'Myles na gCopaleen', made him a national celebrity almost overnight.

Ever since the typescript of *At Swim* went to Longmans, he had been absorbed in a second book which was largely concerned with concepts of Time, infinity and eternity. A few years earlier Devlin had given me a copy of Huysmans' *À Rebours* (much later done into English under the maladroit title, *Against Nature*) and I had passed this on to Brian. He was greatly taken with Huysman's book, and especially with the protagonist, the eccentric aristocrat-philosopher-savant, Des Esseintes. That interest was to be reflected in his creation of de Selby in *The Third Policeman*, though this influence went unnoticed in any reviews I read.

Brian gave me a top-copy typescript of his new book in January or early February of 1940. My first reaction was one of great amusement at the academic battles fought out by those marvellously-named commentators (Hatchjaw, Basset, Le Fournier, du Garbandier, Kraus) in the undergrowth of the footnotes. It was only on a second reading that I realised what a tremendous step Brian had taken into a very different and disturbing region of the imagination.

We move from the hilarious fantasy and high comedy of *At Swim* into a sombre, anonymous landscape, bathed in no earthly light. It is a world of nameless fears, sinister undertones, strange obsessions, the world of Divney and Mathers, the universe of Sergeant Pluck and his molecular bicycles. The typescript was sent to Longmans, but the War had thrown the publishing world into chaos and the book was turned down. Brian was greatly hurt and angered by this rejection. No man of genius is unaware of his quality.

Sometime later he told me that he had mislaid the typescript, probably on a tramcar. He did not say whether a second copy existed, and I didn't ask him, for I had a feeling that he subconsciously wished to 'lose' the book, and, with it, the memory of what he considered to be an unforgivable snub. He rarely mentioned it afterwards, but I am convinced that the text became physically lost, or at least mislaid.

In any event, *The Third Policeman* had to wait twenty-six years for re-discovery and posthumous publication.

In the meantime, he had completed a wonderfully funny book in Gaelic, *An Béal Bocht*, which is considered a classic of modern writing in the Irish language. Unfortunately, it does not lend itself to transla- tion, and there is a curious irony in the fact that he dedicated it to R. M. Smyllie, who could never read it.

'One of the greatest capacities of genius,' wrote T. S. Eliot, 'is the power of development.' Brian displayed this vital, creative power in all his best work, and by the age of thirty he had produced three novels of major stature, breaking new ground every time. His later books— written during the last five years of his life—are remarkable by normal standards, but they can scarcely bear serious comparison with the earlier works.

For some twenty-five years he maintained his 'Myles na gCopaleen' column on a level of wit, invention and intellectual virtuosity that has no parallel in journalism. Did this sustained effort distort his great capacity for development? Did it gradually syphon off his immense reserves of creative energy?

Hemingway, who went through the same mill in his youth, had something to say: 'Journalism, after a point has been reached, can be a daily self-destruction for a serious creative writer.'

Did Brian's brilliant journalistic success and his great popular fame put an intolerable strain on a temperament that was essentially aristocratic, fastidious and private? Had Myles na gCopaleen never existed, would the genius of Flann O'Brien have flowered in other unpredictable masterpieces?

We shall never know.

JOHN GARVIN

Sweetscented Manuscripts

BRIAN O'NOLAN entered the civil service in 1935 and was assigned to the section of the Department of Local Government in which it was my responsibility to supervise the undertaking by local authorities of waterworks and sewerage schemes and to provide for the financing of these undertakings by way of loans and grants from governmental sources. He was aged about twenty-four, smallish, slight, palefaced, with two prominent fore teeth which lent additional sharpness to his oral expressions of mordant wit or vituperation. He quickly picked up a working knowledge of our administration but it took some time to channel his rich linguistic flow within the bounds of objectivity and exactitude and to make him realise that official letters were not an appropriate medium for expressing his personality. Early on I had occasion to require him to excise from a file his record of a conversation of mine with the Parliamentary Secretary (Dr Ward) on a proposal which affected the interests of some of his constituents. O'Nolan wrote: 'Shown to Parliamentary Secretary by Mr Garvin in order to ward off repercussions.'

I was frequently absent in those years on a Tribunal of which I was secretary and O'Nolan was soon able to prepare letters and minute files, leaving them punctiliously prepared for me on my return in the late afternoon.

In 1937 his father dropped dead while playing with his youngest child, leaving a large family poorly provided for. Partly *ex misericordia*, but also on the strength of his ability and efficiency, I recommended his appointment to the vacant post of Private Secretary to the Minister,

Seán T. O'Kelly. He was promoted accordingly and continued to act in this capacity over many years for Mr O'Kelly and his successors, Mr Ruttledge and Mr MacEntee.

Late in 1938 he came to me with a copy of a novel in typescript which he announced had been accepted for publication by Longmans. Slipping into officialese, he said he was submitting it for such general and particular observations as I might wish to offer and for the favour of a Greek quotation to use as an epigraph. He also asked me to consider the title, *At Swim-Two-Birds*, and suggest any alternative that might occur to me.

I read it that night (to coin a cliché) at one sitting. It started with the heading 'Chapter I', but no other chapter heading appeared thereafter. The name of the first person singular narrator was never given. It was soon clear that the 'uncle' who features in the story, like the boy's 'uncle' in Joyce's *Araby*, was in fact the narrator's father.

The washstand ledge in his small bedroom 'contained works ranging from those of Mr Joyce to the widely read books of Mr A. Huxley.' This seemed to be an indirect acknowledgment of his debt to Joyce for a variety of styles of writing (including what a builder would call 'dry filling') and to Huxley for the idea of including in a novel some specialised manuscript material which could be attributed to the authorship of a character in the novel itself, but was otherwise not relevant to the basic plot. Of such material is the lengthy series of stanzas translated from the medieval Gaelic poem, *The Madness of Sweeny*, with which O'Nolan had necessarily to acquaint himself when preparing his M.A. thesis on *Irish Nature Poetry*. His translation, by the way, is not alone very good but also displays in his choice of words a poetic insight into the poetry of the original. There seems also to be a sadistic pleasure in his recital of the woes of Sweeny, a man cursed by a Saint for sacrilege to the end that he was driven to bird-flight and tree-perching all over Ireland.

I read on, through poetry, parody and pub talk until near Lad Lane police station the author and his tall friend, Kelly, met a small man in black who 'talked to me earnestly on the subject of Rousseau. . . . Kelly then made a low noise and opened his mouth and covered the small man from shoulder to knee with a coating of unpleasant buff-coloured puke.'

A similar gastronomic reaction is suggested for Mr Furriskey, a character created (and brought alive) by Trellis the author about whom the narrator is writing. Furriskey's 'drinking capacity, speaking roughly and making allowance for discrepancies in strength as between the products of various houses, was six bottles of stout and any quantity taken in excess of such six bottles would not be retained.'

The concluding part of the book, omitting filling-in stuff such as how to read the gas meter, etc., seemed very good. Some of the passages detailing the cruel revenge taken by Trellis's rebellious characters on their author were extremely well written and betrayed the pleasure which the writer took in thinking up various forms of torture. The Pooka Mac Phellimey politely announces to Trellis the treatment to which he is to be subjected:

It is my mission here this morning to introduce you to a wide variety of physical scourges, torments and piteous blood-sweats . . . boils upon the back, a burst eye-ball, a leg-withering chill, thorn-harrowed earlobes . . . an anabasis of arrow-points beneath the agnail, razor-cut to knee-rear, an oak-stirk in the nipple, suspension by nose-ring, three motions of a cross-cut athwart the back, rat-bite at twilight. . . .

Next day Brian came in to my office, took note of his offspring at my elbow, and awaited my verdict with an affectation of the diffidence which he showed in submitting official papers. I praised his achievement in artistically synthesizing such a variety of themes and styles. I said that the title would puzzle the non-Irish reader, but it seemed adequately explained in the body of the volume as a translation of *Snámh Dá Ean*, the historic ford on the Shannon at Cluan Mhic Nóis. Then, again, an exotic work like this should have an exotic title. However, an alternative had occurred to me when I came to the unfortunate little man in black at Lad Lane: perhaps he might consider calling the book *Sweetscented Manuscript*?

My suggestion was rewarded with a smile but capped by an alternative alternative from the author—*Longman's Folly*. I made some suggestions for minor revisions in the interest of clarity and I gave him a quotation from the Greek.

The following spring *At Swim-Two-Birds* appeared in black hardboard with title and author's pen name, Flann O'Brien, engraved in gold upon the spine. Longmans' reader, Graham Greene, himself a writer of whose merits we were then unaware, praised the book but *The Observer* reviewer, Frank Swinnerton, did not appreciate its phantasies and criticised the juvenile character of the prose in such passages as that already quoted about Mr Furriskey's capacity for stout. Later that week in March, 1939, Brian sent me an envelope posted to him from Greystones, containing a tin nameplate from a railway station slot machine, on which some fervent partisan had punched 'F. SWINNERTON'.

Brian's literary triumph was duly celebrated. He and I left the office together and in the Palace Bar we joined Bertie Smyllie and Alec Newman of the *Irish Times*. From a neighbouring table Austin Clarke said that O'Nolan 'had fallen in with tradition' and quoted *the saint-bell of saints with sainty saints*. I murmured that Clarke himself would make a nice twin for Sweeny in the Trees. Pussy O'Mahony came out of the snug that was there then in the back room and joined us. I asked him what would he have and he said nothing, that he carried his drink around with him, proceeding to take a glass of whiskey out of his waistcoat pocket. 'Anything,' he said, 'to escape that ranter O'Riordan, ex-D.I., R.I.C., out of Battersby's in the snug in there, boasting of all the I.R.A. men he saved from the Black-and-Tans.' Alec McCabe, from somewhere behind me, said that O'Riordan was a bloody liar, 'and you know it, John'. Then Smyllie reverted to what was, apparently, his previous theme—the rape of Czechoslovakia and the lunatic exultation on the power-crazed Führer's face as he gazed from an eminence upon the beauties of Prague. I noticed that Brian had grown silent, withdrawn into himself behind a toothy grimace, his melancholy eyes contemplating the vacuum of his glass abhorrently. He perked up a bit when I ordered a fresh round of drinks and more so when Alec Newman, who was Trinity scholar in classics, enquired where he got the Greek quotation facing the alleged 'Chapter I', ἐξίσταται γὰρ πάντ' ἀπ' ἀλλήλων δίχα.

'I mean to say it's unusual, you know, finding a classical quotation used as an epigraph with no indication of its source.'

'There's the source, so far as I'm concerned,' Brian said, indicating me.

'Don't heed him,' I said, 'he got it from his friends Timothy Danaos and Dona Ferentes, the two Greek characters in his book.'

'But seriously, John,' Alec said, 'why make a mystery of the thing? A thing, you know, that should be on record.'

I gave chapter and verse, I said: 'They must have fallen off the page in sick transit: Euripides, *Hercules Furens*, in consideration of the corresponding agony of Frenzied Sweeny; and the verse itself, "For all things go out and give place one to another", in relation to the rapid succession of characters and plots right through the novel.'

'Oh, I see,' Alec said, 'Existatai—*Exeunt omnes*. I see now.'

'They all go out,' Brian said, 'when the skivvy burns the MS. that sustains their existence. John made me make this explicit—he is a devil for keeping you meticulously bloody accurate.'

About a year afterwards on my way back from lunch I met Brian at O'Connell Bridge and we walked to the office together. He said that he had written another book—and lost it! He took it in to the Dolphin Hotel the previous night to show it to a fellow and what with one thing after another, he went home without it.

'I'm after being down there, had them beat the whole bloody building and sight or light of it's not to be found.'

I commiserated with him and enquired as to the nature of the work. He entered on his account of it eagerly:

'I have a policeman using his spare time in his station creating unnatural devices—a small, beautifully made chest containing a similar but smaller chest which is the receptacle for one still more diminutive and so on in a series which ends with one nearly half a size smaller than ordinary invisibility; a leprechaun's piano whose notes are of such high frequencies that they cannot be heard by any human ear but the inventor's; a spear which draws blood at six inches' distance from its visible point; and a colour hitherto unknown to human eye which makes all who see it blind madmen.'

This book, *The Third Policeman*, was found and published in 1967 —after Brian's death. The phantasy in it is more tightly drawn than that in *Swim-Two-Birds*. Analysis of it reveals it to be hell for all eternity where the damned soul goes round in circles which repeat themselves without any recollection on the victim's part of his having made the same circuit already. This hell is a part of Ireland, more or less un-peopled, save for the elementals who staff it—three policemen, two of whom are also attending a mechanized purgatory devised by the *Third*, Constable Fox. The police were a class to which Brian was allergic and here Flann O'Brien is at it again, presiding over an Inferno run by his dearest enemies—'The Rozzers'. The landscape in which the pathetic prisoner persists, pending his hanging, is marvellously por-trayed as is the condemned one's ideas of his life after death.

In 1948 I became Secretary of the Department and Brian Ó Nualláin, who used this Irish version of his name in the office, was an Assistant Principal Officer. He was, also in 1948, promoted Principal Officer of the Roads Section but only in an acting capacity because he refused to attend before the Chief Medical Officer to have himself medically examined as a check on his sick-leave record. He had by this time made his name, i.e. the name of Myles na gCopaleen, as a columnist in the *Irish Times*. When he was good he was very, very good. I recall his account of a nightmare in which he gropes in the dusty top of the wardrobe and brings down an old, dirty violin case, takes out a handsome, red instrument of great age; soon a dreadful wail pierces the night. Tosselli's Serenata. Unearthly music late at night, a lepre-chaun's tiny orchestra scares homing drunk passing outside in the frost. 'I awake in the cold morning . . . casually bring chair to wardrobe, mount it, have a look. No violin. Nothing but a dust-caked coat hanger.'

The joy of living which lightened the rigour of his early writings was, however, giving way to a more sombre outlook on the world. Wit and humour were subordinated to subserve censure and satire. A series of articles about Senator Andrew Clarkin, a kindly merchant, Lord Mayor of Dublin, 1951–3, was heralded by the slogan 'ACCISS!'. It appeared that this meant *Andy Clarkin's Clock Is Still Stopped*, which in fact was and continued to be the case outside his coal office in

Pearse Street. But some of us knew that Clarkin relied largely on his intelligent and charming wife ('Cis') for advice on difficult problems posed by his duties as Lord Mayor and that Myles's cabbalistic formula really meant 'Aks Cis'. In 1953 a new national festival, An Tostal, was inaugurated and, concurrently, Marshal Tito of Yugoslavia visited Britain. Myles mentioned the possibility of a member of Dublin Corporation being questioned about Tito's coming to Dublin for the Tostal and replying that that horse wouldn't stand a chance in any race short of four mile. But perhaps he might be backed on the Titostalisator? At this, the councillor's mouth falls open, revealing graveyard of sunken teeth, and the malt-eroded voice says 'Wha-a-a???' The remainder of the article was an attack on the Senator and his alleged shortcomings in mayoral hospitality: who ever saw the froth of his pint? O'Nolan was by this time Principal Officer of the Planning Section, a post which entailed correspondence on highly controversial issues, particularly in Dublin, and he was widely known in this capacity, apart altogether from his journalistic fame. The dichotomy in his responsibilities in these two fields could not be sustained indefinitely and in 1953 he retired on pension from the public service on the ground of ill health. A short time previously he had assured me that his income was limited only by the amount of time he saw fit to devote to his writing.

I do not recall having ever discussed with Brian the origin of his pen-name, Flann O'Brien, but I was and am quite certain that he derived it from the hero of an old ballad, Brian O Lynn, in Irish, Brian O Fhloinn, which he turned backways, taking the nominative of O Floinn, Flann, as a personal name which, indeed, it was—one thousand years previously. Frank O'Connor remarked that the name looked like an Easter egg with a Santa Claus beard on it. The ballad was humorous after the mid-nineteenth-century fashion:

> Brian O'Lynn, his wife and wife's mother
> Were all going over the bridge together
> The bridge broke down and they all fell in—
> We'll go home by water, says Brian O'Lynn.

Brian O'Nolan had a hotted-up modern version of the ballad to which he treated some staid clerks celebrating a promotion. They called him 'a bowsey', a Dublin term for anybody who acts out of keeping with the character of the society in which he finds himself. They were, of course, right, their songs being usually of the Moore's melodies type or respectable drinking songs such as that beginning *In cellar cool*. Brian, for his part, had as much contempt for his bourgeois assistants as he had for the civil service overlords with striped trousers in the corridors of power whom he stigmatized as 'Kerry peasants in Treasury pants'.

Over his period of eighteen years in the Civil Service, Brian kept up a constant and delightful correspondence with me, sending me letters from illiterates, nitwits and 'quare fellas' with appropriate comments. When I was dealing with the supervision of home assistance administration he wrote enquiring whether I would regard the figures on the Parthenon frieze as coming within the statutory definition of outdoor relief. Conversely, he adopted some of my bilingual phrases such as 'deinde out' (day in, day out).

I once told him that I did not consider him a good critic of his own work because he tended in the one book or even in one article to vary his style from well-knit, recondite prose to sterile word-play and inane conversation pieces.

He replied that he could not argue on the point as he never re-read his published works, but that he had fans for all his different presentations—some readers thought his Keats and Chapman pre-fabs were the last word, while others entreated him to give them more of The Brother. He went on to point out that James Joyce, who had scarcely vision enough to pursue his own writing, had put up an observatory of glasses round his face in order to read *At Swim-Two-Birds*.

It is true that Joyce considered Flann O'Brien to be a great comic writer but it would seem that it was the technique of *At Swim-Two-Birds* and its author's ideas of the novelist's functions which really caught Joyce's attention. The only portion marked in Joyce's presentation copy of the book is the page which contains the statement, 'that a satisfactory novel should be a self-evident sham to which the reader could regulate at will the degree of his credulity'.

JACK WHITE

Myles, Flann and Brian

MYLES NA GOPALEEN sprang fully-grown from the brain of Brian O'Nolan in the autumn of the year 1940; and for about a quarter of a century his 'Cruiskeen Lawn' appeared, with erratic regularity, in the *Irish Times*. No other writer in his class, so far as I know, has produced a daily newspaper column: certainly no other has written in this form so much of his best, his most original, and his most influential work. The influence of Myles was pervasive precisely because his writings appeared in this ephemeral form. Through the columns of the newspaper which was read by most literate Dubliners, the work of Myles na Gopaleen was able to irrigate their minds and their speech.

Brian O'Nolan made his first recorded appearance in the *Irish Times* by way of the 'Letters to the Editor'. In December, 1938, a new play by Frank O'Connor under the title *Time's Pocket* was presented at the Abbey Theatre. It was lambasted by the critics: O'Connor's friend and fellow-Corkman, Sean O'Faolain, rushed in to lambaste the critics. Brian O'Nolan (over the signature Flann O'Brien) then weighed in to lambaste O'Faolain with a fierce and funny letter which ended: 'What Mr O'Faolain wants is a sound spanking—that, or five minutes with Mr Sears [the drama critic of the *Irish Independent*] or myself behind the fives court.'

The controversy ran for some weeks, with a variety of contributors, many of them writing over pseudonyms: Niall Sheridan played a number of parts. Sheridan recalls that he then introduced Brian O'Nolan to the Editor of the *Irish Times*, R. M. Smyllie, and that Smyllie had the inspired idea of inviting this erudite jester to contribute a regular column in Irish to the newspaper.

Memory must have abridged a time-lag here, I think. The first contribution that I can find under the heading 'Cruiskeen Lawn' did not appear until 4th October, 1940, and then over the by-line 'From a Correspondent'. The article took as its text a recent leading article on the Irish language which ended: 'Has Gaelic ingenuity for that matter stretched so far as to provide a really expressive and indigenous equivalent for the well-known "Axis"?' The smug paternalism of such comments, securely based on ignorance, would have brought the blood of any old-time Gaelic Leaguer to boiling point. The Correspondent, much more subtly, turns the leader to ridicule, by constructing around it a crazy conversation between a Gaeltacht mother and her son.

About a week or so later the column begins to appear more or less regularly, over the signature Myles na gCopaleen.* Generally it was in Irish and in the Gaelic script, but sometimes it was in English, or in Irish roman type. It provoked a very early reaction from *Irish Times* readers. On 17th October, a letter signed 'West Briton Nationalist' took the Editor severely to task: 'I do not understand what worthy motive can inspire your "skits" on the Gaelic language and its students as such. It sounds very like fouling one's own nest. I have heard many adverse comments on Irish. But you are spewing on it.' Another anonymous reader charged that: 'You are following a set policy in an attempt to sabotage (as they say nowadays) the propagation of the language and things Irish.' And a Mr Jack O'Neill suggested that a feature in Irish would be welcome 'provided it were on sensible topics and written by someone obviously not embittered. . . . Fun and humour are to be welcomed in such a column, but there is no fun in hitting below the belt.'

But the attacks were more than balanced by letters from readers who were delighted with the new feature. 'Is it possible,' asked one,

* The original form of the pseudonym was Myles na gCopaleen. It was taken, in a spirit of mocking paddyism, from Boucicault's *The Colleen Bawn* (which derives from Gerald Griffin's novel *The Collegians*). The change to Myles na Gopaleen was made, I think, after he had begun to gain some celebrity outside Ireland, in deference to the Anglo-Saxon epiglottis. We in the *Irish Times* cherished the pedantry of the eclipsis in the genitive, but he had his way.

'that we are producing a Gaelic Stephen Leacock?' '"Cruiskeen Lawn" endears itself by its mature humour and its graceful diction', writes another. A reader who signs himself 'Eamonn an Cnuic' writes: 'Far from poking fun at our native tongue, Myles has ably demonstrated its elasticity and adaptability . . . I hope the spicy breeze of Myles's humour will help to clear away "the mist that does be on the bog" from modern Gaelic writings.'

The most significant comment, perhaps, came from P. O. hAodha, who wrote that he did not wish to take sides in the argument, but: 'I have been reading (or looking through) the Irish that is printed in our newspapers for many years, and I do not remember having ever seen an article which called forth a single comment, be it praise or blame, from the readers. That should be a sufficient defence for your contributor—if indeed he needs any.'

This instant reaction must have given great satisfaction to the Editor. To set the language enthusiasts at each other's throats, and to do it by way of a column in impeccable Irish, was the kind of success that would have delighted Smyllie's sense of humour—even though he was unable to read a word of it himself.

It was often said of R. M. Smyllie that he was the last of the great editors. He was an editor, that is, in the sense that Louis XIV was a king: an editor by divine right, an absolute tyrant, an editor who left the imprint of his personality all over his newspaper. At this time he was about fifty; he had been editor for six years, and he was at the height of his hegemony. The position he occupied in Dublin society is illustrated in a celebrated cartoon by Alan Reeve which depicted the Palace Bar in 1940. Almost every writer and artist then practising in Dublin is included, and Smyllie's place is in the centre.

In a country with only three national newspapers, no weekly press of any intellectual standing, and only a sporadic mushroom-crop of literary periodicals, Smyllie's *Irish Times* occupied a position of rare significance. It was traditionally Protestant, traditionally conservative, traditionally pro-British; and Smyllie himself shared most of these attitudes. But the very fact that the paper held a minority position gave it a degree of independence that Smyllie was able to exploit. In matters of social policy the conservative ground was occupied, for the most part, by the Catholic Church. The *Irish Independent* was traditionally deferential to the Church; the *Irish Press* was the organ of the Government party. The *Irish Times* was the only organ free to be reformist, if not radical, in its social policies. For years it ran a persistent campaign against the Censorship of Publications Board, which was then in the heyday of its pursuit of the Indecent and Obscene. (There was even a school of thought which held that it was improper to publish the official list of books banned by the Censors, lest the prurient reader be enticed into seeking them out.) 'The *Irish Times*,' wrote Vivian Mercier a few years later (*The Bell*, January 1945), 'is ten times more alive than its rivals in the newspaper world. . . . the *Times* is always ready with a campaign, a controversy, or an appeal—V.D., T.B., Post-War Planning, The Abbey Theatre, the European Relief Fund. The other papers must sometimes envy the *Irish Times* its fun, if not its circulation.'

The comment was perceptive: Smyllie enjoyed being an editor. He enjoyed gathering writers about him, as company and as contributors; he enjoyed being able to extend them a modest patronage—the odd guinea for a book review, or couple of guineas for a poem. 'The Saturday Book Page of the *Irish Times*,' Mercier wrote, 'is now the only real focus for Dublin's writers outside this magazine.' It appealed to Smyllie's sense of fun to engage a columnist whose first contribution was a send-up of one of his own leaders. 'Does any other paper in the world allow its editorials to be parodied right on the editorial page?' asks Mercier. 'Beachcomber's or Low's disrespect for their several employers is as nothing compared with Myles na gCopaleen's. It goes without saying that no Irish paper except the *Times* would print a Gaelic column so unorthodox as Myles's.'

The first 'Cruiskeen Lawn' appeared just at the time when the first great air-raids of the War hit London. The *Irish Times* then retained more or less its pre-War format, and it reflected an Ireland that was still barely touched by the War. Stirrup-pumps for A.R.P. were advertised in the front page, but pictures of the day's race meetings and social events occupied the back. By 1942, when I joined the editorial staff, the paper was down to four pages a day, and news had finally replaced the advertisements on the front page. But, even under the severest pressure on space, 'Cruiskeen Lawn' retained its half-column in the leader page. By now it had become one of the most prized features of the newspaper, and its author was a celebrity. In 1941 he had published *An Béal Bocht*, dedicated to 'my friend R. M. Smyllie'* and established himself as the most original of contemporary writers in Irish. The exploits of The Brother were followed in every pub, and the in-tray carried a monotonous stream of letters from correspondents anxious to contribute to the Keats-Chapman cycle.

The circulation in those days never ran much above 30,000, and almost all of this was in Dublin. Some country newsagents, indeed, refused even to handle the 'West British' paper. (They would never have sold more than a couple of copies a day anyway, so they could afford to indulge their principles.) On the other hand the paper could claim a 'quality' readership—professional people, upper civil servants and businessmen—and it exercised an influence out of proportion to its sales.

I have by me a little anthology of *Cruiskeen Lawn* published by Cahills (undated, but the National Library lists it as 1943). It is printed in two parallel columns of Irish and English, probably (to judge from the type-setting) from the original *Irish Times* galleys. Even by war-time standards it is a sorry enough job of book-making, but it gives a fair sample of the Myles of the mid-War period. Here are Keats and Chapman, developed long past the early investigations into Chapman's Homer; here are the Plain People of Ireland, tirelessly poking in their snout; here are the fantasies built around old engravings; here are the assaults on the citadels of Culture—the ballet, the Institute for Advanced Studies, the National Gallery:

---

* The dedication reads: 'Do mo chara R. M. SMYLLIE: R. M. O Smaoille, .i. An Smaolach.' The word *smaolach* means thrush. In Smyllie's own copy Myles had added with a pen the gloss: *turdus magnus*.

Seventy-five per cent of the pictures in the National Gallery are fakes. The next time you are there take a penknife to the fine El Greco and scrape away a square inch of the picture where your handiwork will be least noticed. You will come across a banner painted for the 1903 Irish Language Procession in Wexford, in which my uncle had the distinction of riding the first bicycle ever made in Ireland . . .

Initially, Myles was commissioned to write three times a week in Irish. But the great majority of readers could not read Irish, and before long they began to feel that they were missing something. So the commission was stepped up to six articles a week, three in Irish and three in English. After a time the proportion of Irish began to decline, and by 1945 an article in Irish was a rarity. This was not a matter of editorial policy; in fact, Smyllie was very keen to keep on teasing the Gaelic-Leaguers, and he tried to insist that Myles should produce his quota of Irish; but in practice Myles did as he pleased. Perhaps he found Irish harder work; perhaps the performer was responding to the larger audience.

The reaction of the audience should be taken into account in any assessment of Myles na Gopaleen. Academic critics, not surprisingly, tend to feel sympathy for a writer producing six columns a week under pressure of a deadline. The strain must indeed have been considerable; but it should be recognized, too, that the writer in a daily newspaper is in close and constant contact with his readers and can establish a much more intimate relationship with them than the author of books. Myles could hand in a column in typescript on Sunday evening, and go into a pub where people were chuckling over it on Tuesday morning. In effect he was able to keep up a dialogue with his audience, absorbing the reactions into the next work to be produced. He had available to him, too, that favourite device of the comedian, the cumulative effect. Keats and Chapman became funnier as the cycle went on, because the audience knew the game; and so he could even cheat for effect—as in the episode of Mr Childs and the trip to India (*BoM*, p. 195). Later on, I feel, he came to interpret this instant reaction as influence, or even power.

By 1942, when I first came to know him, Myles had reached the height of his comic powers, and he poured the whole of his antic genius into 'Cruiskeen Lawn'. I imagine that he saw it, at that time, as no more than a short interlude in his writing career. The War was not an encouraging time for a new writer, especially one of his re-markably original talents. His first book, *At Swim-Two-Birds*, had been published in 1939 and, in spite of a good reception from critics, it was virtually swept away by the tide of war. *An Béal Bocht* (1941) was recognized as a masterpiece, but only by the relatively limited audience open to a book in Irish. There was talk of another novel, irretrievably lost. Indeed I was given a circumstantial account of this calamity. He had been on a motoring tour with a friend, the story went, in Co. Donegal; the manuscript was lying loose in the boot of the car; at every stop the boot was opened, and the wild winds of the North whipped away a page or two, until the entire novel had vanished page by page over the Bloody Foreland. I never thought I was expected to believe this yarn; I just assumed, as everyone else did, that he had never managed to write the second novel at all. What none of us knew, of course, was that *The Third Policeman* had been rejected by Longmans, and that he had hidden it away. To reveal such a disap-pointment would have humiliated him, I suppose, before the crowd in the Palace: like any Irishman, he would rather be a clown than a failure.

Ireland in the War years had need of a satirist. The isolationism of the Thirties, followed by the real isolation of the War, had turned the country into a cultural reservation, cut off from the nurture and stimu-lus provided by influences from abroad. Dublin Corporation had just distinguished itself by refusing to hang a picture by Rouault in the Municipal Gallery, on the ground that the representation of Christ was irreverent (the picture found a home in St Patrick's College, Maynooth); while the Censorship Board, turning aside momentarily from its task of cutting a swathe through international literature, had placed its ban on a racy but innocent collection of folk-chat from Cork, *The Tailor and Ansty*.

In these topical controversies Myles affected (if it was an affectation) the role of the impatient pedagogue. In his comment on the Rouault affair, he rakes with his grapeshot not only the Corporation and Sean Keating, the academician, but 'our own pathetic and untidy advance guards who have never learnt to draw'. His pretension was to put down all pretensions; and, in the role of the crotchety pedant, he hammered the knuckles of writers, artists and critics alike (see almost any piece in *BoM*, 'Criticism', 'Art', 'Letters'). His broadsides were much enjoyed—Dubliners delight in the discomfiture of others, especially their friends—but it would be unsafe to accept his judgments at face value. Of one of his favourite targets, *The Bell* (edited by Sean O'Faolain), Dr J. H. Whyte has written: '*The Bell* during its years of existence kept liberal criticism of Irish society alive until . . . in the fifties a more open climate of opinion began to emerge in Ireland.'

A study of 'Cruiskeen Lawn' at this period, indeed, reveals little observation of Irish life that would have been beyond the range of a man sitting in a pub with the morning newspaper; and as a picture of the learned author this is probably not very far from the truth. At a time when most of his contemporaries were married and had homes of their own, he was still living the life of a bachelor. Women, it may be noted, figure rarely in the column, and when they do appear they occupy a stock role, like 'the wife' in comic postcards. His own ear and eye were tuned mainly to the population of the public-houses. His mastery of speech-patterns is a constant delight to the knowing reader: from the monotony of pub-talk he has contrived something funny and fantastic.

He is at his best when he counterpoints lunatic invention with the flatness of demotic Dublinese. Look at his speculation on the nature of the 'strange little animal' that frequents the house (*BoM*, pp. 105–6), with interruptions from the Plain People of Ireland, who conclude with the advice: 'Show that badger the door. Chinaman or no Chinaman.' Or study the exquisite absurdity of the court hearing (*BoM*, p. 122) in which the defendant is charged with being under the influence of intoxicating ice-cream.

We paid him, if my memory is correct, at the rate of two guineas an article, of about 500 words. But this was two guineas per article *printed*, and the rate of rejection was high. His copy usually arrived in batches of two or three articles at a time, typed on foolscap paper (Government issue). One of the duties of the junior in the editorial department was to sub the copy and read the proofs. Copy was scrutinized for libel, scurrility and double-meanings: columns that offended were chopped ruthlessly or thrown into the wastepaper basket.

With nearly every batch of copy there was a covering letter, generally a fearful outburst of invective against the 'cornerboys' (a favourite word) who had allowed typographical errors to appear in the column, or who had disallowed some of the previous week's contributions. In terms of sheer scurrilous abuse I have never seen anything quite like those letters. Eventually Smyllie conceded a point: he arranged that Myles was to be paid on the basis of columns submitted, whether printed or not.

All this time he was still a full-time civil servant in the Department of Local Government. It was a source of some wonder to us that he managed to lead this double-life. There is evidence that, as time went on, Myles na Gopaleen began to invade the office of Brian O'Nolan. A colleague recalls seeing him, in the private room which he enjoyed after his promotion to Assistant Principal, engaged in transcribing the letters of Lord Chesterfield, to fill the column on an arid day; and when he finally left the Department his successor found in his desk an old Victorian encyclopaedia with most of its engravings cut out, to provide the raw material for the Myles na Gopaleen Research Bureau. Eventually, it was the entanglement of his two careers that led to his retirement from the Civil Service.

In 1951 Fianna Fail came back to office after a three-year break, and Patrick Smith was appointed Minister for Local Government. Smith was a tough Cavan man, very different from the previous Ministers under whom Myles had worked—the suave Sean MacEntee and the easy-going Sean T. O'Kelly. About this time Myles was carrying on his campaign against members of Dublin Corporation; in particular, he was engaged in harrying the Lord Mayor, Andy Clarkin. While the clock over Clarkin's office, for some reason, stayed stopped, Myles mounted an all-out campaign for its repair. He ran a series of columns under the heading ACCISS—signifying ANDY CLARKIN'S CLOCK IS STILL STOPPED—and he tried to mobilise readers to give Clarkin the ACCISS salute, holding one arm up and the other out horizontally, like the hands of the clock. It was not a very brilliant joke at any stage, and Myles carried it to the point of persecution. He even persuaded the Editor to spread it through the columns of the newspaper. The victim complained, but Smyllie took no notice. Presumably he then carried his complaint to the Minister.

Myles had always boasted (it was an aspect of his *folie de grandeur*) that no connection could ever be proved between Myles na Gopaleen and Brian O'Nolan. If any Minister tried to penalize him for his writings, he claimed, he would bring an action for wrongful dismissal, and challenge the Minister in court to prove that Myles and Brian were the same man. Smith was not the man to be deterred by such niceties. He gave an order that Brian O'Nolan was to be fired. But sacking an established civil servant is a complicated business, beyond the powers of an individual Minister. In the end (principally, I believe, due to the intervention of John Garvin, then Secretary of the Department) it was arranged that Myles would be permitted to retire on partial pension, on grounds of ill-health.

Retirement from the Civil Service must have been a landmark in his life. He had achieved the freedom that most part-time writers dream about—the freedom to leave other work behind and write as a professional. But he had left behind, too, the discipline of regular employment, regular hours, regular colleagues: a discipline which never seems to have constricted him very much. It is possible that his release came too late. It did not mean liberation: it meant that he was condemned for the rest of his life to the newspaper treadmill.

I do not know anything about his financial circumstances, but drinking at Myles's level is an expensive pastime; and in his later years he must have had recurrent hospital bills. He was never well paid by the *Irish Times* (nobody was: the paper was poor, not mean). So he began to turn his hand to casual journalism. About the end of 1954 he offered

71

a regular column to the *Southern Star*, Skibbereen. The proprietor, Mr O'Regan, liked the sample article, and contracted for a weekly column. It was published through 1955 and 1956, under the heading: *A WEEKLY LOOK ROUND, by John James Doe*. Most of it consisted of a fairly pedestrian commentary on the week's affairs: no doubt he was aiming consciously at a rural readership (I can see him playing to the national xenophobia when he writes darkly: 'I believe half of the radio musicians in Dublin and Belfast are foreigners'). I think it possible that he conceived of this column as a syndicated feature, running in a number of local newspapers: it seems unlikely that he would have singled out one small paper in Co. Cork for such an offer. But, if this theory is right, there seem to have been no other takers.

Later on, about 1960, he proposed a weekly column to Liam Bergin, the Editor of the *Carlow Nationalist*, who had been a good friend of his for a number of years. 'We had a discussion about the subject matter', Bergin writes, 'and finally I thought it better to give him a free hand. He decided that it would be better not to write under his own or any of the already known assumed names. Having given some thought to this he decided on the name George Knowall. The material was good, usually at somewhat greater length than he wrote for the *Irish Times*. I always remember that he was meticulous about meeting his deadlines. Of course there were gaps of two or three weeks at times when, for various reasons, he was "out of commission".' The column ran for five or six years, up to the time of his death.

He contributed as well to *Sunday Review*, a tabloid published by the *Irish Times* (the *Irish Times* was intended to live on its immoral earnings, but the *Review* ended up living on the moral earnings of the *Irish Times*): for this column he used the name Matt Duffy. And for about two years in the Fifties he wrote a weekly column for the Irish edition of the *Sunday Dispatch*: as Myles na Gopaleen, of course, since the *Dispatch* was interested in buying the name. A colleague who worked in the Manchester office, which was responsible for the Irish edition, recalls that the feature was dropped because he began to send in copy in Irish. Copy was often late anyway, turning up on Saturday instead of Thursday, and nobody had time by then to go out and seek for a translation. Not surprisingly, the Northern Editor refused to take a chance on publishing copy that nobody in the office could understand. There is a strange perversity, in this context, about his stubborn refusal to go back to writing Irish for the *Irish Times*.

I went to London for the *Irish Times* just after the War, and when I came back, after six years, I found a great change both in the Editor and in his star contributor. Smyllie had always been a hard drinker: by 1952 his health was poor, he was in and out of hospital, and his judgment, always arbitrary, had become increasingly erratic (he died two years later). Myles, just turned forty, was wearing badly; he had become cantankerous and he bitterly resented editorial interference. Rows developed between him and Smyllie, and Myles began to flourish his resignation.

By this stage he had become bored with The Brother and with the lively fantasies that made his early work so enjoyable. He saw himself more in the role of a latter-day Swift, with the mission of chastising the folly and hypocrisy of contemporary Ireland. A vindictive streak in his writings led to constant problems with the paper. Again and again copy was rejected because of attacks on his favourite targets—among them his former Minister, Sean MacEntee, and the Secretary of his old Department, John Garvin: both, as we understood, men who had shown him considerable generosity.

Nothing made Myles more furious than to have his copy chopped for fear of legal action. He took extravagant pride in his ability to circumvent the law of libel; and in fact he attracted singularly few actions, considering the nature of his material. But apologies sometimes had to be made. The Directors of the Abbey Theatre extracted an apology from the paper for a column which implied that they were lining their own pockets out of the State grant to the theatre; and there was, I believe, a threat of action from the Institute for Advanced Studies. I rely on memory here, since I have been unable to document the affair, but I believe that the threat arose from an article in which Myles linked two learned papers by scholars of the Institute; a philosophical discourse by Professor Erwin Schroedinger on 'Science and

Humanism', and a paper by Professor T. F. O'Rahilly which set forth the proposition that two different missionaries to Ireland had been confused under the name of St Patrick. The Institute, Myles said, had succeeded in proving that 'there were two St Patricks and no God'. It was a neat sally, and much repeated around Dublin; but Dr O'Rahilly was not amused.

The rejection of copy led to rows, and more than once Myles announced his positively last appearance. The Board, I think, would have seen him go with no regrets: they found him something of an embarrassment. But the readers missed their 'Cruiskeen Lawn', and something had to be done. Since I was Features Editor Myles was my responsibility, and in fact we had always remained on friendly terms, even when he was at odds with the paper. So I had to go out to find him and get him back.

At this time he was living near me, in Blackrock, and even my children were familiar with the drab little figure in the pork-pie hat who could be seen passing down the road, with the marionette-step of the habitual drinker, on the way to get a curative gin at Gleeson's as soon as the doors opened. In one of his pieces for the *Southern Star*, in 1955, he wrote: 'My hat is disgracefully aged. Its useful life is long since over. It is stained. It is no exaggeration to say it is filthy. But its many years of faithful service has [*sic*] turned it into part of me. To a large extent, I have become myself simply something that fits in under the hat.' It is an oddly accurate sketch: the hat seemed to overshadow and almost extinguish his small, rather secretive face. The portrait head of him by Sean O'Sullivan, used as frontispiece to this volume, seems strangely naked without this dingy crown.

By nature, I think, he was a quiet, rather introverted person; in drink he became extravagant and even bombastic. I remember that, on one of my diplomatic missions, when we went back to his house, he confided to me that he had it in his power to make a revelation that would blow the entire Irish language movement sky-high. It is hard to believe that he himself took this kind of bragging seriously. It was a performance, which had to be staged, even for an audience of one.

Our last meeting was in his bungalow at Stillorgan, a year or so before he died. I had moved into television in 1961 and had more or less lost touch with him. James Plunkett, then a television producer, conceived the idea of getting Myles to write a series of dialogue sketches for that great comedian, Jimmy O'Dea. With some patience, he assembled the series, set in a railway signal-box, which Jimmy performed (with David Kelly) under the title 'O'Dea's Your Man'. It must have been from James Plunkett that I heard that Myles was in bed with a broken thumb, and I went out to see him.

He was sitting up in bed, with the hand bandaged. He spent most of the visit explaining how he was going to recover a vast sum in damages for his injury. He had spent a morning (I think it was Christmas Eve) in Phil Byrne's at Galloping Green. He intended, he said, to spend the afternoon in bed working, and he looked around for some harmless beverage to relieve his thirst. His eye lit on a bottle of orange squash, so he bought it and took it home. All afternoon he sat in bed, working away, and refreshing himself from time to time with a swig of orange squash, until at last he finished the bottle. At this point he found it necessary to get out of bed; whereupon he fell flat on the floor and broke his thumb. It was obvious, he pointed out, that he had been poisoned by the orange squash. How could this happen? Because, in simple ignorance, he was drinking the stuff *undiluted*! He had studied the label, and there was no word of warning that water must be added. Obviously neat orange squash was toxic; the makers were guilty of negligence, and he was going to sue for such monumental damages that they would have to shut up shop for good. He was so entertained by his own effrontery that he kept bursting into sputters of laughter.

He was difficult company in those later years. The resentment that always lay close below the surface seemed to rise up and find expression in outbursts of scorn that no longer distinguished between the humbug and genuine. Too much contempt had soured his palate. He rarely revealed himself in enthusiasm or praise. We in the *Irish Times* thought he was a scholar *manqué*, and there is a rare note of sincerity in a generous appreciation which he wrote to mark the twenty-fifth anniversary of the death of Standish Hayes O'Grady, Editor of *Silva*

Gadelica: 'He combined with profound learning other qualities of humour and imagination which enabled him to deal with early texts in a lively creative way that lifted his work far out of the repellent rut traversed by most philologists.' Given another lifetime, this might have been his own obituary.

He was fond of scoffing at the Americans, scholars and thesis-writers, who came to Dublin as pilgrims on the trail of James Joyce. 'Perhaps the true fascination of Joyce,' he wrote in *Envoy* (April 1951), 'lies in his secretiveness, his ambiguity (his polyguity perhaps?), his leg-pulling, his dishonesties, his technical skill, his attraction for Americans.' As I write this I have beside me a letter from an Italian student who is coming to Dublin to pursue a thesis on Myles na Gopaleen. What, I wonder, would the Plain People of Ireland have said to that?

J. C. C. MAYS

Brian O'Nolan: Literalist of the Imagination

BRIAN O'NOLAN came of age in a literary as well as literal sense in the 1930s. Only *At Swim-Two-Birds* was published at the time, at the end of the decade, but the other three novels in English published after a long interval of more than twenty years only make it more obvious that he looked backwards for the establishment of his literary identity. Again, though all four English novels were first published outside Ireland, all four depend on a sense of the quite specific Anglo-Irish literary dilemma of that time.

Samuel Beckett[1] described the alternatives facing the Anglo-Irish poet in the thirties as a choice between 'antiquarians and others, the former in the majority'. He contrasted the Twilighters, who proceed from 'the *Gossoons Wunderhorn* of that Irish Romantic Arnim-Brentano combination, Sir Samuel Ferguson and Standish O'Grady', with those noticed by Yeats as 'the fish that lie gasping on the strand'. He took the second and smaller group, who looked abroad for models to aid their perception and expression of life as it is, to 'constitute already the nucleus of a living poetic in Ireland'. The analysis can perhaps now be admitted a remarkably astute one and it is relevant, with few modifications, beyond the situation in verse. The alternatives in prose may be said to have been pointed to by Liam O'Flaherty and by Joyce, either to unsling the camera and follow across the dreary plain[2] or to look abroad to the master of silence, exile and punning. Characteristically, Brian O'Nolan continued to see the alternatives as falsely opposed and yet as inescapable.

Brian O'Nolan's attitude to any simple-minded literary nationalism of the Daniel Corkery kind is made clear on a number of occasions, most amusingly in the parodies of *At Swim-Two-Birds* and *An Béal Bocht* and most explicitly in the columns of 'Cruiskeen Lawn':

> This trouble probably began with Lever and Lover. But I always think that in Synge we have the virus isolated and recognisable. Here is stuff that anybody who knows the Ireland referred to simply will not have. It is not that Synge made people less worthy or nastier, or even better than they are, but he brought forward with the utmost solemnity amusing clowns talking a sub-language of their own and bade us take them very seriously. . . . That comic ghoul with his wakes and mugs of porter should be destroyed finally and forever. . . . [*BoM*, pp. 234–5, 234][3]

Brian O'Nolan's attitude towards Joyce is considerably more admiring. He sent an inscribed copy of *At Swim-Two-Birds* to Joyce in Paris (with '*diffidence*')[4] and praised him across the whole span of the 'Cruiskeen Lawn' columns—in 1944 as being with Yeats the only Irish literary figure not a 'literary vermin, an eruption of literary scabies', and in 1962 as being 'of more general world significance than either Yeats or Shaw' (CL, 1st September, 1944; 26th July, 1962). He praised Joyce's 'almost supernatural skill in conveying Dublin dialogue' (CL, 6th June, 1957) and his humour above all else: 'the true fascination of Joyce lies in his secretiveness, his ambiguity (his polyguity, perhaps?), his leg-pulling, his dishonesties, his technical skill, his attraction for Americans. His works are a garden in which some of us may play. [All that we can claim to know is] merely a small bit of that garden.'[5] If we had missed it before, the sting is in the tail, the hit at Joyce's overweening pretensions as an artist and God-rivalling 'tourdeforcity'. In *The Dalkey Archive* the Joycean figure of De Selby presides over a paradisal 'vestibule of a heavenly conspection', attempting with monstrous arrogance to cramp magnificence into philosophical (Viconian) patterns (*DA*, pp. 7–8). 'One who reduced the entire literary world to a state of chronic and helpless exegesis' (CL, 12th September, 1949), the undoubtedly high-minded Joyce also shows an 'exceptional lack of moral judgment'.[6]

If both alternatives are to be rejected, the grounds for rejection are different in each case, which is important. Brian O'Nolan heaped scorn

on the ritually conceived link between literary and political identity
that had sustained the Revival. An urban writer from the North, he
had little sympathy for the cosy cottage-industry ideal of a Hy-Brazil
'Corkadorky'. Like most writers of his time, when early revolutionary
hopes had waned and 'obscurantism had settled on the country like a
fog',[7] he was not much inclined to be inspired by crude appeals to
Catholic conscience or by over-indulgence in nostalgic nationalism.
Even so, he did accept the basic ordinary values involved at a human
level in a way which those who left Ireland felt they could not. 'The
only good thing about the Diplomatic Corps is that it enables you to
get out of Ireland', Denis Devlin told Mervyn Wall,[8] but, after a brief
sojourn in Cologne, Brian O'Nolan returned to join the Department
of Local Government. What he found admissible and even necessary
to him in a fundamental way in the Ireland of the Thirties is characteristically difficult to demonstrate unless by contrast with his view of
Joyce, whom he appears to have recognized as the most dazzling of
stars in the contemporary literary firmament, but in the end unsound.
Joyce is inevitably to be preferred on the level of artistry, but on the
level of day-to-day and time-to-eternity living Brian O'Nolan looks
for his values nearer home. The narrator of *At Swim-Two-Birds* has
books by Aldous Huxley alongside books by Joyce on his washstand
shelf (*AS2B*, p. 12), and the following passage from Philip Quarles's
notebook in *Point Counter Point* describes Brian O'Nolan's own attitude towards the Master:

One of the hardest things to remember is that a man's merit in one
sphere is no guarantee of his merit in another. Newton's mathematics
don't prove his theology. Faraday was right about electricity, but not
about Sandemanism. Plato wrote marvellously well, and that's why
people still go on believing in his pernicious philosophy. Tolstoy was
an excellent novelist; but that's no reason for regarding his ideas
about morality as anything but detestable, or for feeling anything
but contempt for his aesthetics, his sociology and his religion. . . . it's
obvious that excessive development of the purely mental functions
leads to atrophy of all the rest.[9]

On the one hand, 'Your men of this *United Irishman* interpret freedom as a system whereby the fancies of clods are to be imposed by force on everybody'; on the other, Brian O'Nolan asks, 'Could the man of parts live without grocers?'[10]

Samuel Beckett has been cited on the alternatives facing Irish writers like Brian O'Nolan and himself in the Thirties, and it happens that Joyce[11] set *At Swim-Two-Birds* and *Murphy* against one another as 'Jean qui rit' against 'Jean qui pleure'. The comparison pursued in the two writers' divergent reactions to Joyce's example makes Brian O'Nolan's position clear. Beckett's reaction to Joyce's mastery and artistry is a consciousness of what, despite all the achievement can encompass, is necessarily omitted: 'The more Joyce knew the more he could. He's tending towards omniscience and omnipotence as an artist. I'm working with impotence, ignorance.'[12] Brian O'Nolan's criticism is less aesthetic and more moral, and grows in severity with time. The narrator of *The Third Policeman* indulges a De Selby-MacCruiskeen inspired speculation of infinite regression, and the conclusion is intended forcibly to cast doubt on the process that led to it:

A body with another body inside it in turn, thousands of such bodies within each other like the skins of an onion, receding to some unimaginable ultimum? Was I in turn merely a link in a vast sequence of imponderable beings, the world I knew merely the interior of the being whose inner voice I myself was? Who or what was the core and what monster in what world was the final uncontained colossus? God? Nothing? [*3P*, p. 118]

What for Beckett is a dilemma, fidelity to which makes a new kind of anguished success ('the heart of the cauliflower or the ideal core of the onion would represent a more appropriate tribute to the labours of poetical excavation than the crown of bay'),[13] is for Brian O'Nolan both inviting and presumptuous. Joyce's world is one in which he delights, for its obeyance only of its own fantastic laws and its appearance of liberation from all dull customary physical restraints; and yet one wherein he conceives art has stepped beyond its prerogatives and lost its hold on reality, which is only too successful as a temptation from the proper path. The divergence is clearly apparent in a comparison of *Murphy*'s Celia with *The Dalkey Archive*'s Mary, who occupy a similar position in relation to the protagonist of each novel. Whereas for Beckett love and affection and ordinary values are given as a temptation which must be overcome on the journey towards the un-attainable 'little world' of Mr Endon, for Brian O'Nolan these ordinary values are departed from only at risk, though the temptation is always to take it. Brian O'Nolan's faith in any Magdalen Mental Mercyseat is not ironic, and however he indulges the directionless self-negating tumult of his wit it is never the way salvation lies. The paradox is that his early writing, in which his consciousness of moral perspectives serves only to maintain the purity of the fantasy, in fact achieves Beckett's stated ideal more completely than anything Beckett himself has written. The narrator of *At Swim-Two-Birds* withdraws his 'powers of sensual perception' and retires Oblomov-like (complete with stye) into the kingdom of his mind, where there is 'complete darkness and an absence of movement on the part of the cerebral mechanism' (*AS2B*, pp. 9, 15) and where he in fact attains Murphy's third 'dark' zone. What more perfect embodiment of Murphy's 'matrix of surds'—'a flux of forms, a perpetual coming together and falling asunder of forms'[14]—than the whole of *At Swim-Two-Birds*?

On the one hand, therefore, is Brian O'Nolan the artist delighting in elaboration and intricacy and humorous effect, on the other is Brian O'Nolan the moralist communicating his distaste for pretension and pride, and artist and moralist combine in various ways in his writing with various success. The counterpointing is undoubtedly most perfect in the two early novels and the newspaper column which followed them and which is collected in *The Best of Myles*. Each of the three books in its own way preserves the peculiar impersonal balance between ordinariness and vertiginious extravagance that is Brian O'Nolan's inspiration as a writer. Each of them locates its art firmly in a moral context, which yet only serves to prevent the norm of fantasy from degenerating into self-congratulation and to preserve its extraordinary purity. In suggesting that it is misleading to say Brian O'Nolan was a born writer 'if craven dedication to trade is implied', Niall Mont-gomery[15] also suggests that Brian O'Nolan's great 'common touch' and indifference to the seductions of art make him instead a sorcerer, 'owner of a cauldron out of which he pulled words, common and uncommon, to clap, like scalding pitch-caps, on the shrinking heads of concepts happy hitherto to be nameless'. In Brian O'Nolan's later writing the fine balance is upset; his impetuous and somewhat intimidating commitment to ordinary virtues usurps the achievement of the earlier books and makes it of a different sort altogether. The Stephen Dedalus figure in the novels bows to the values of Bloom, as before, but the extraordinary celebration of the ordinary world characteristically becomes less extraordinary. At times it becomes insistently commonplace (as in many later 'Cruiskeen Lawn' columns), at times even sentimental (as in Mick's relation to his mother in *The Dalkey Archive*, or in the character of Mary). When the later writing succeeds it is on the different grounds of its harder cruder force, although this itself sometimes degenerates into waspish resentment. Brian O'Nolan's theme in *At Swim-Two-Birds* has been described as 'The imagination is wrong and leads to suffering: a simple art-free life is best.'[16] The description is wrong not just because the opposition is too crude, which John Wain himself recognizes, but because it ignores the opposition's mainspring and preservative. Brian O'Nolan's manner at its most dazzling is Trellis-like, De Selbean, and when it is not the result is *The Hard Life*. The moral frame, at the same time, is quite otherwise. It is merely a perspective on the manner, a necessary and liberating framework to fantasy. When such an inevitably precarious relation grew to be defined as stark opposition, art inevitably lost to life, and perhaps life lost something also.

The position of 'homebased exile'[17] was lonely but congenial, and to an extent contrived. It is inevitable that the sources of Brian O'Nolan's inspiration should be idiosyncratic or perversely commonplace, that he should discover humour in Standish O'Grady's footnotes and irrepressible breeziness in his scholarship[18] or that a Quaker Oats advertisement should be the most likely inspiration for Policeman MacCruiskeen's boxes.[19] Equally inevitable is that the deepest sources of his inspiration should be negative. He is centrally in the mood of his generation of Irishmen in reading *Ulysses* as a legpull and *Finnegans Wake* as the ultimate fantasy in cod.[20] *The Dalkey Archive*'s presentation of Joyce as the author of pamphlets for the Catholic Truth Society of Ireland merely develops Michael Lennon's wounding suggestion[21] that Joyce might have a more rewarding future in such a role; perhaps it owes something also to Lennox Robinson's early play, *The Lost Leader*, in which Joyce's hero Parnell is presented as living on as porter in a small West of Ireland hotel, and which the Abbey had revived during the Thirties. Again, much of the parody of low Dublin voices in *At Swim-Two-Birds*, 'Cruiskeen Lawn', *The Hard Life* and so on is described by Richard Ellmann's definition of a Bloomism as 'an uneasy but scrupulous recollection of a factual near-miss',[22] or is clearly inspired by certain of the later stories in *Dubliners* and the Cyclops episode in *Ulysses*. None the less, if 'Strong basement smells assailed his nostrils' (*AS2B*, p. 43) is a sentence which could not have been written without Bloom,[23] Brian O'Nolan's employment of the style is not only as distanced as Joyce's but calculated in a different way. Dublin in the Thirties seemed like 'an inferior plagiarism from *Ulysses*',[24] and Brian O'Nolan took the joke further than anyone else; yet, as Joyce's reputation and influence spread, Brian O'Nolan reacted the more wholeheartedly against it. When reviewers of the republished *At Swim-Two-Birds*[25] associated him with Joyce, his renunciation grew even to be savage. In similar fashion, *The Third Policeman* makes use of J.-K. Huysmans' *À Rebours*, a use which places it in a tradition of Anglo-Irish writing including also George Moore's *A Mere Accident* and *Mike Fletcher* and Oscar Wilde's *Dorian Grey*, but Brian O'Nolan's use of Huysmans attempts wholly to deny Huysmans' values. *The Third Policeman* likewise makes use of the writing of J. W. Dunne (*An Experiment in Time*, *The Serial Universe*, etc.), writing which had been cited with approval by several Irish writers of the time like the brothers Yeats, but again his use is negative.

Certainly it is relevant that a turn was given to Brian O'Nolan's writing by such events in his life as Longmans' rejection of the *Third Policeman* manuscript (which affected him deeply and in ways that are not fully apparent in his writing for some time afterwards) and by R. M. Smyllie's invitation to write for the *Irish Times*, but such events were fortuitous. Certainly a novel like *At Swim-Two-Birds* can be placed centrally in a tradition in modern literature which also includes Pirandello's plays and *Les Faux-Monnayeurs*.[26] Elizabeth Sewall[27] has pointed out how the nonsense world of Edward Lear and Lewis Carroll makes the same attempt to render language a closed and consistent system of its own, which is the aesthetic of modernism—a coincidence which Brian O'Nolan had begun to exploit to the full some years before. Again, however, the coincidences are largely fortuitous, and the literary historian is likely to have more need of them than did the author. Like several others at the time—like Eimar O'Duffy in *King Goshawk and the Birds* and Brinsley MacNamara in *The Various Lives of Marcus Igoe* a few years before, or like Mervyn Wall and Austin Clarke in their Celtic-Romanesque romances a few years afterwards, or Jack B. Yeats—Brian O'Nolan pursued a vein of fantasy, but in his own inimitable way and for his own private reasons. He was never a member of a significant group or conscious movement—he wrote for *The Bell* as well as for *Ireland Today*—and what views he shared with friends like Niall Sheridan and Niall Montgomery are less important than his almost necessary sense of separateness. The only source of inspiration he acknowledged without qualification—though he took care to define it in his own idiosyncratic way—was the native Irish tradition for which he had a genuine love, and typically on the grounds of its uselessness and total separation from modern concerns. His M.A. thesis on nature in Irish poetry was on a subject with clear and fundamental attraction for him, but, characteristically, from all reports it was impeccably academic.

As a writer whose roots lie in the Ireland of the 1930's, Brian O'Nolan is in the end his own man. The combination of sheer ordinariness and sheer unpredictable fantasy is a paradox protected by privacy. Each of his *personae* at different times allowed different scope to his genius, but the attraction of his writing is also founded on the sense of something withheld and quite separate. We are struck by an intrinsic fastidiousness or reticence which involves mingled pride and humility, and which has little in common with the self-indulgent blether and boisterous farce of some of his latter-day admirers. It is a quality that colours all aspects of his writing, large and small, from the characteristic form of his sentences to the way in which he manipulates plot, and that enables the writing to be at its best mocking and humane, austere and extravagant, committed and shy, compassionate and gay, all this and more at the very same time. It encourages affection as well as respect. What delights and persuades in Brian O'Nolan's writing is ultimately a range of human qualities, paradoxical as it may seem when what is best in it is most impersonal.

*   *   *

At Swim-Two-Birds was a long time in the making. It was begun during Brian O'Nolan's last year in College and during the years that followed it grew to many times the length of the book we have now. The original version was, according to Niall Sheridan,[28] less a book than a territory to which Brian O'Nolan retreated to develop as he would a multitude of themes that interested him. These origins account for the book's essential character, which is that of a compendium of anecdotes and competing voices. The way in which a degree of order was imposed on this marvellous but unwieldy thing was first of all not only by savage pruning, but by pruning which isolated a number of unifying structural motifs.

What remains in the book as we have it are three main plots—as the narrator remarks at the opening and close, he has a particular fondness for threes.[29] First there is the story of the narrator himself, his life at home with his uncle and as a student at University College; second, there are his occasional ventures into the legendary world of Finn McCool and the Frenzy of Sweeny; and last there are his incursions into the fictional world of Dermot Trellis. All three plots move at speeds appropriate to the worlds they inhabit. The frame story moves carefully through the seasons of the narrator's final undergraduate year; by contrast the Finn story is timeless, recurring through the book as if at random and with minimal progression; the Trellis story moves between the two, and though there are gaps in its telling which are filled by synopses, only once is a scene presented out of sequence. None the less, if so much is clear, these matters are less clear actually in their working out. The effect of three narratives moving forward at an unsynchronized pace and at different removes of sympathy from the author who stands behind them, the movement from one world to another unprepared, the insertion of extracts drawn from such random sources as Falconer's *Shipwreck* and a forty-volume *Conspectus of the Arts and Natural Sciences*, in particular the complications and inversions of the Trellis plot, is of a swirling phantasmagoria in which a great deal of movement is accompanied by less advance.

The narrator's comment on his handling of the Trellis story is to be taken seriously, whatever reaction it provokes in Brinsley. He argues that 'a satisfactory novel should be a self-evident sham to which the reader could regulate at will the degree of his credulity' (*AS2B*, p. 33). Characters are to be allowed 'a private life, self-determination and a decent standard of living' and should be 'interchangeable as between one book and another'. The argument describes the 'aestho-autogamy' or 'aestho-psycho-eugenics' on which the conflict between Trellis and his characters rests. However, it is not the idea in itself which makes up the character of the book, but how it is developed. Characters possess not only an independent existence which can be carried over from one book to another, but they move from one to another of the three plots of the same book. *At Swim-Two-Birds* is the 'work of reference' the narrator claims a modern novel should be, but in a more extended sense than is sometimes understood. There is an elusive but persistent relation established between the author-narrator so attracted to 'the tender trestle of [his] bed' (*AS2B*, p. 15), with his stye, and the flabby, pimply, bed-habiting author Trellis. An equally real if more elusive relation comes to be established between Trellis and Sweeny: in one version of Orlick's story towards the close of the book, the House-Moling who had before served Sweeny becomes the cleric Moling who clambers into Trellis's room (cf. *AS2B*, pp. 125, 238), in another Sweeny's initial crime is duplicated by Trellis (cf. *AS2B*, pp. 25, 118, 246), in another Sweeny the Kite of Cluain-Eo is reborn as the thorn-embedded tree-benighted Trellis—Sweeny is made to 'live in tree-tops and roost in the middle of a yew' as Trellis is set 'at his bird's roost on a thin branch surrounded by tufts of piercing thorns and tangles of bitter spiky brambles' (*AS2B*, pp. 25, 265). Other characters and scenes are at the same time made curiously to echo one another, with a similar unsettling effect. Various details of the meeting over which the uncle presides and at which the narrator acts as secretary are picked up in the trial of Trellis, which again includes details from previous bar-scenes involving the narrator and his companions; Orlick's style inevitably recalls Finn's, Shanahan's recalls Kelly's, that of the Ringsend cowboys recalls faintly but unmistakably that of the College students (the oblique parallels extending here even to the matching of heating systems in the College and in an ideal ranch-house and to a penchant for pyromania).

This is the effect of the book as a whole and the point of its epigraph from the *Hercules furens*. If it is highly contrived, with plots set against counterplots, and styles against styles and parodies of styles, the balance so made up is not static. The counterpoint method is such that any connection between the parts of the book frustrates another at the same time that it establishes itself: 'all things fleet and yield each other place'. The effect of this method of counterpoint is in the end to communicate a fantastic imagination of a peculiar sort. The real subject of the book is vigorous ingenuity, wildness and sweetness, those qualities of the legendary Brother Barnabas and other *personae* which Brian O'Nolan's friends remember at their most unrestrained in his College years and in the years immediately following. Such satire, Niall Montgomery has written,[30] springs up 'not out of bitterness but from helpless, disbelieving enjoyment of the perverse fantasy of conventional behaviour'. Private jokes contribute to the mood, even when they are impenetrable. Cashel Byrne is the poetaster-painter Cecil ffrench-Salkeld, for instance, but who is the small man Kelly covers with buff-coloured puke, whom Brendan Behan[31] claimed to have identified? It does not matter. Failure to assimilate totally the book's material is likewise paraded as attraction, and the relevance of the *Athenian Oracle* and other extracts to any of the plots is often remote.*

* This is not to deny that seemingly arbitrary details do not yield up a significance. Heine's *Die Harzreise*, which the narrator wants to buy but never gets round to buying, deals with students, is full of puns and epigrams, shifts to fairy-tales, legends, descriptions of nature, etc., in much the same way as *At Swim-Two-Birds*.

An anonymous grammarian interjects the names of figures of speech; there are nonchalant lists, broken-off *resumés*, interrupted reminiscences, inadequately impersonal descriptions, detailed interpretations of motive and conduct which confuse more than they illuminate. Gratuity relished is the essence of this extraordinarily contrived book, and its variety is overwhelming. As the Good Fairy comments, 'Counterpoint is an odd number . . . and it is a great art that can evolve a fifth Excellence from four Futilities' (*AS2B*, p. 156).

There is of course a serious substrate to the humour of *At Swim-Two-Birds* which, without in any way giving the book a moral, prevents the whole fabric from collapsing upon itself in sheer facetiousness. A norm is asserted not only in the unerring openness and energy of the book's approach to its material but also in the shaping of the material. In the framing plot the narrator emerges from his involvement with Trellis to see his uncle and the ordinary world in the end not ungratefully; a certain pride and selfish indulgence gives way to an awareness of and generosity towards others. Again, as we grow in familiarity with the book and come to have a sense of it as a whole, we realize that the first extract from the narrator's Finn typescript is given where it is, out of sequence at the beginning and before the narrator's first experience of intoxicating beverages, because it stands as prologue. Finn, the weaver of a story-teller's book-web, prefigures both Trellis and Orlick, both the villain and also the person by whom the villain is ultimately vanquished. Who but a story-teller to introduce a story which concerns ill-usage at the hands of and eventual triumph over a story-teller by a story-teller for a story-teller? Finn is the least satirized of the three narrators of the three stories; his world of the out-of-bed outdoors is a parodied but still live and affectionately observed world. His songs—as a comparison with their middle Irish originals[32] will reveal—have little or no parody in them. Lamont's dismissal of them as 'your fancy kiss my hand' and Shanahan's preference of 'A Pint of Plain is Your Only Man' (*AS2B*, pp. 110, 112–13) are as overt a statement as Brian O'Nolan comes to make on the values they embody, but again it is significant that the longest of the Finn episodes in which they appear is the turning-point of the book.

The exact relevance of these matters is defined by the title *At Swim-Two-Birds*. On the one hand the title is suitably gratuitous, being merely one of the many places visited by Sweeny ('on a Friday, to speak precisely'); on the other it is a place where, at a church beside the Shannon opposite Clonmacnois, where cultural and religious values were for a spell coincident in a darkened Europe, 'the clerics were engaged at the observation of their nones, flax was being beaten and here and there a woman was giving birth to a child' (*AS2B*, p. 95). Brian O'Nolan translates literally and without mockery from the *Buile Suibhne* here, and the lay that Sweeny sang there is at the centre of the positive values in the book. Quite properly he does not include it, but similar values are embodied in the following uncollected poem translated from the Irish:[33]

> Here's a song—
> stags give tongue
> winter snows
> summer goes.
>
> High cold blow
> sun is low
> brief his day
> seas give spray.
>
> Fern clumps redden
> shapes are hidden
> wildgeese raise
> wonted cries.
>
> Cold now girds
> wings of birds
> icy time—
> that's my rime.

At Swim-Two-Birds is Brian O'Nolan's Brother Barnabas book. His contributions to *Comhthrom Féinne* and to *Blather* are perforce more talked about than read, but the book writes out at large the same ever-renewing energy delighted in for itself that has passed into legend. This is where its centre lies and, though its construction is intricate, it gives little sense of shape. What shape it has was largely discovered in the process of bringing a semblance of order to the unorderable, as distinct from a shape either imposed or consciously built upon. The exercise of preparing *At Swim-Two-Birds* for publication was not without benefit, and Brian O'Nolan's next book was composed very much more quickly on the basis of what he learned.

The evolution of the method of *The Third Policeman* from that of *At Swim-Two-Birds* is clear. The relation between the parts of the later book is, because designed from the first, more obvious. The cast of characters is reduced, the range of parody is restricted, and the loosely related plots of different kinds are now stacked within one another snugly, like a nest of tables. Characters continue to merge into one another—the one-legged men and Policeman Fox into Mathers, most obviously, but both of them partially into the controlling, contriving narrator just as the pub merges into the barracks into Mathers's house, the narrator into De Selby into Policeman MacCruiskeen. The merging of one thing, person and place into another in the later book is, then, with a more limited purpose and with a correspondingly stronger single effect; it is as if the whole of *At Swim-Two-Birds* had narrowed to the Trellis plot, absorbing the narrative frame and jettisoning Finn. The mirage of correspondences of *At Swim-Two-Birds* in this way becomes an unalleviated nightmare of infinite recession. Another significant change is that this counterpoint is a quality that not only we the readers are aware of, but one that the narrator himself is solipsistically aware of too. Whereas the Pookah and Furriskey had defined the opposing limits of action for the characters themselves in the previous book, Martin Finnucane and Joe are now restricted to the narrator's world. He himself is neglectful, idle, bedloving as before; he creates the same sort of world as Trellis's, whose laws differ from those of the normal world and yet are strictly controlled; but the result is now circular, macabre, hellish. The norm of fantasy is tinged with the grotesque.

The differences between the two books undoubtedly derive from a particular clear apprehension of moral implications in the earlier one, and to these everything is subordinated. In *The Third Policeman*, with the exception of the first and last framing chapters and two others, each chapter is contrived to open with a meditation on De Selby from which in elusive and oblique ways the rest follows. The chapter in which Mathers's house becomes his coffin follows on from De Selby's cogitations on the house as box, the chapter in which the evil genius Martin Finnucane establishes claims to companionship and gives directions as to how to reach the barracks follows on from De Selby on roads which encourage you in whatever direction you are already travelling, and that these ideas have also become the narrator's assumptions is revealed as the plot develops. In Chapters VI and X, which are not introduced by reflections on De Selby, we on both occasions learn of how Fox was crazed by MacCruiskeen. The event is as carefully dated as the narrator's entrance into the world of De Selby and reminds us that the third policeman contains the two first just as the narrator of the whole book moves within a universe of De Selby. The book's progress on the level of style and parody is identical. De Selby's manner is repeated in that of his commentators and of the commentators on his commentators in footnotes, and it creates the world in which the narrator moves. If he appears to go beyond it, into an outdoor world of ordinary things like bicycles and lanes and fields and policemen, or to have escaped from the scaffold, he continues deluded. The narrator who speaks in Chapters VI and X does not speak with his own voice, but again in the voice of another, be it Sergeant Pluck or another un-named. And Sergeant Pluck himself, in Chapter VI, merely takes over the manner of Martin Finnucane, which in its turn is only a special instance of De Selbean rhetoric at a lower level of control. Structure and style in this way come to mirror a vision of infinite recession which appals, fascinates and amuses, resting as it does on an ultimate assertion of unmitigated selfhood. The book's method is its theme: the dizzying indulgence in the abyss of selfhood (*der selbe*), the regardless pursuit of omniscience (*omnium*). A narrator whose thoughts were 'never far from De Selby', that is, from one who likewise held that the 'usual processes of living were illusory' and for whom he committed his first serious sin and his greatest sin (3P, pp. 92, 9), ends counterfeiting infinity, forging the quintessence of 'business-end of everything'—'Some people call it God.' (3P, pp. 110–11.)

The nature of Brian O'Nolan's theme can be appreciated more clearly with reference to his major source, if that is the word, Huysmans' À Rebours. MacCruiskeen, with his 'dark Jewish face and hooky nose and masses of black curly hair' (3P, p. 57) and his habit of swearing unless he is a Dutchman (3P, pp. 67, 111), is an ironic counterpart to the creator of Des Esseintes. Old Mathers's colour theory centring on blackness takes off from Des Esseintes' theories, which in turn centre on the famous episode of the black meal in the opening chapter of À Rebours:[34] as a central and one of Huysmans' most memorable images of inversion, this last echoes through The Third Policeman, from the epigraph's mention of 'black air' to the opening words of the final chapter—'The night seemed to have reached its middle point of intensity and the darkness was now much darker than before.' (3P, p. 193.) De Selby's travel-theory is a little changed borrowing from Des Esseintes';[35] MacCruiskeen's light-mangle is only a transposition into other senses of Des Esseintes' symphony of liqueurs;[36] De Selby's 'hydraulic elysium' plagiarises the 'appareils hydrothérapiques' in Des Esseintes' dressing-room.[37] The attention given to left-turning roads and left-mounted bicycles and left wooden legs is again not fortuitous, they are emblematically à rebours. Nor is the attention given to teeth, those hostages to time and human frailty in both books: 'Nearly every sickness is from the teeth', repeats Sergeant Pluck (3P, pp. 54, 199), and we recall the horrifying humiliating instance of nature's revenge on Des Esseintes at the hands of the dentist.[38] The point is, though, that what for Huysmans was a world to be created and explored as a thing to be sought after is for Brian O'Nolan a thing of fascination but also of folly. 'Since the affairs of men rest so uncertain', his second epigraph runs, 'Let's reason with the worst that may befall'. Huysmans' artificial world makes up an image of self—whether a God-rivalling artist's like Joyce's, or a scientist's like Einstein's, or a philosopher's like J. W. Dunne's—which Brian O'Nolan makes his own and rejects.

If the details and the inspiration are often similar, therefore, the interpretation is not. What is presented in all seriousness by Huysmans becomes the occasion for both humour and horror. It is important to recognize that Brian O'Nolan's subject is not so much evil as folly, which makes his book of a different kind from Huysmans' even if Huysmans' is read as a satire. The narrator of *The Third Policeman* is not wholly bad; though he commits every sin, there is some vestige of goodness in him. His ride on the stolen bicycle to escape from the barracks is, for instance, presented in terms of an adulterous liaison. 'How desirable her seat was, how charming the invitation of her slim encircling handle-arms, how unaccountably competent and reassuring her pump resting warmly against her rear thigh!' (*3P*, p. 171.) But the liaison has a very real warmth and considerable humanity. When we follow it through its stages, we share the narrator's feelings almost completely. If we need to judge the narrator it is more for his foolishness in accepting the Sergeant's theory of the intercommunion of molecules, his absurd contribution to the mystery of the body and spirit and of incarnation which results in the transference of sex and humanity to machines. The narrator may be blind but he is not felt to be wicked. We are touched by the way he is comforted by the reappearance of the adulterous bike: 'Something slipped gently into my right hand. It was the grip of a handlebar—*her* handlebar. It seemed to come to me out of the dark like a child stretching out its hand for guidance.' (*3P*, p. 193.) And we are touched even more if it crosses our minds, as it is surely meant to, that his accomplice had only too willingly been away deceiving him the while under another rider. In a similar way, there is more pathetic inadequacy than *fin de siècle* sickness in the narrator's Bloom-like visions of an *omnium* utopia (*3P*, pp. 189–90).

The Third Policeman is indeed distinguished by the extent to which we are placed within its action as we read it. Everything is self-created, has its own laws given it by boundless invention, we share the exhilaration of 'using our imagination' as the narrator is so often told to do; yet we are trapped within a self-spun web, imprisoned in an infinite hall of mirrors. Everything has a claustrophobic double-sidedness. Three carefully charted days are sixteen undeniable years. We move from place to place and meet person after person, and yet all is evolved from the dreamer's mind. The nature that the narrator escapes to only mirrors his thoughts. For example, the contrast between MacCruiskeen hunched over impossible objects too small to be discerned and men working 'diminutively in the distant bog, toiling in the brown turf and heather' (*3P*, p. 125) at first strikes us with relief; that is, until we realize that the narrator's senses are supernaturally alert to interpret the genial day only for his benefit, that the earth is being seen in its turn only as a great workshop selfishly to be made use of. The weather, the surroundings, nothing is taken on its own terms; it is only taken conditionally, to confirm a feeling or as an occasion for self-gratulation. The scaffold is under construction: 'Black quails called sharply from their hidings and a swollen stream was babbling dementedly. Trees, I knew, would be angular and ill-tempered in the rain and boulders would gleam coldly at the eye.' (*3P*, p. 148.) O'Feersa has gone to fetch the one-legged men to rescue the narrator: 'A bird sang solo from nearby, a cunning blackbird in a dark hedge giving thanks in his native language. I listened and agreed with him completely.' (*3P*, p. 151.) The most innocent and charming scenes turn out to be unreal projections—'the fine views of bogland had been arranged by wise hands for the pleasing picture they made' (*3P*, p. 37)—or impositions usurping reality. 'Trees were arranged here and there with far-from-usual consideration for the fastidious eye'; 'The house was quiet in itself and silent but a canopy of lazy smoke had been erected over the chimney to indicate that people were within engaged on tasks.' (*3P*, pp. 39, 86).

The characters are similarly all puppets. If we are at first reassured by the enormous burly forms of the policemen, we nearly choke, as the narrator does, when Sergeant Pluck taps his forehead to produce 'a booming hollow sound, slightly tinny, as if he had tapped an empty watering-can with his nail' (*3P*, p. 154). In the end, of course, we realize it is true that he is only 'a toy man' (*3P*, p. 163), just as Mac-Cruiskeen is only 'a walking emporium . . . on wires and worked with steam' (*3P*, p. 76). Little is clear about Fox 'except his overbearing policemanship, his massive rearing of wide strengthy flesh, his domination and his unimpeachable reality' (*3P*, p. 180), yet he is the least credible. But if he is the least present of the three, as well, he is for that reason the least illusory, closest to the centre of the book and most fit to give the book its title. The narrator, despite his sense that the life 'bubbling at the end of [his] fingers was real and nearly painful in intensity' (*3P*, p. 102), is dead, nameless.

The creation of a world which is demonstrably false, at which we can therefore laugh and yet from which we cannot escape, is the source of *The Third Policeman*'s strange magnetic attraction. It achieves Des Esseintes' ideal of hallucination through artifice, the substitution of 'le rêve de la réalité à la réalité même', but it does so to a different end. Brian O'Nolan's end is not anguish but fantasy, not the exotic and the perverse but the unbelievable proved, not neurosis but a world exhilarating and wrong.

The Best of Myles is Brian O'Nolan's third major piece of writing. It is the second book-length selection to be made from the 'Cruiskeen Lawn' column and the first to be widely circulated. It was never conceived of by him as a book; even so, it may well prove to be his most widely popular. The origins of the column are described elsewhere in this volume. What is of interest at this point is the scope it afforded Brian O'Nolan's talents as a writer, and the relation it bears to his novels.

The *persona* of Myles na gCopaleen is an opportunistic adoption prompted by the Ascendancy affiliations of the *Irish Times*. Its literal origins in various nineteenth-century sources do little more than situate a latter-day Shaugraun in his traditional context, and the *persona* there located is inconsequently inconsistent. The family background of Sir Myles na gCopaleen (the da), which reads like a parody of so many Big House novels, is a strange one for Myles himself, 'the brilliant young journalist', and it is difficult to follow the relation of a father who celebrated his eighty-seventh birthday in the 1940's to a son who was able to fight for 'full regulator' practice on Irish railways in the 1880's (*BoM*, pp. 154, 348). The *persona* is carefully established—his wife, his house on the N.C.R., his work as railwayman and journalist, his comings and goings assailed by the man with the Brother, the man with the Watch, the man with the Blade—but it is at the same time not surprising that the Myles na gCopaleen Research Bureau is also a pool of hacks (disused National Teachers and others) who are to be held reponsible for the various literary productions. The Myles-ian or Nagcoplian *persona* (*BoM*, p. 250) offered Brian O'Nolan not so much a particular fixed point of view from which to appraise various aspects of contemporary folly as, instead, a means of variously developing his fine wit, regardless of consequence. Indicative of the freedom encouraged by the new *persona* is the frequency of punning and word-play, which is elsewhere unusually infrequent in a writer so intoxicated with words.

There are grounds for assuming that the 'Cruiskeen Lawn' column is to an extent satirical. Brian O'Nolan makes plain the snobbish pretensions of so many Gate theatre patrons and the dullness of the Abbey, he mocks the stereotyped professional Irishman and language buff, he points up the autodidactic idiocy of the Brother and his equally idiotic and gullible admirers, he explodes stereotypes and *clichés* in thinking, feeling and expression. As one might have expected from his assault on human pride in *At Swim-Two-Birds* and *The Third Policeman*, his opposition increases to match the pretensions of folly. Though no person or group is altogether spared, he has clearly less patience with the 'dainty, sherry-sodden coyness' of the 'gombeen-bourgeoisie' (*BoM*, pp. 257, 248) than with, say, 'a certain modest Dublin man with nothing but a Synge Street education' (*BoM*, p. 246). Poor Paud may not be delicate or winsome but at least he escapes the dire fate of being 'gracious' and the strain of distaste in Brian O'Nolan's parodies of aesthetes is as certain as the relish in his parodies of the Plain People of Ireland. In his assaults on the former the Myles-ian mask indeed occasionally slips, and when we read 'Let there be no more of this nonsense' (*BoM*, p. 239) we take it that he believes what he says. However, when the satirical strain has been isolated in such a way it becomes clear that this is not where the attraction of the writing lies. Brian O'Nolan's readers would be very many fewer if such considerations were foremost in their minds, since the values the writing upholds are not unusual, and at times ordinary to the extent of being reductive, simplistic, obscurantist. When he writes about the innovative giants of the cinema, that 'for all the long words and scratched sepia negatives they are a lot of small boys if you compare them with the men on the coast' (*BoM*, p. 246), he writes ironically in the style of an ignorant demagogue; but equally, his sympathy for the audiences of the second sort of film is the greater for their not being disfigured by 'the drop of red wine and the pot of French mustard' (*BoM*, p. 247). There is at times, and not only in the later years of the column which have not been collected, a too great readiness to allow impatience with coteries and cults to overtake fair judgment on what they have attached themselves to. The writing is not sustained by the sense of standards upheld against the inroads of egocentricity and pretension but by its sheer impersonal liveliness.

If *The Best of Myles* is satire, then, it is so in Chesterton's sense of being 'a variation or fantasia upon the air of pure logic'. The sources of its attraction lie not in our moral awareness of some folly exposed but in the way folly is conceived as absurdity, and the absurdity is drawn out and isolated for all to see and relish. The method is self-generating; W.A.A.M.A. creates the opportunity for *buchhandlung*, which is extended in the ventriloqual escort service. We read with a blank mind at first, but it quickly becomes attuned to the logic of taunting reasonableness which gathers manic speed. In the Keats-Chapman series the build-up is to a startlingly literal and practical letdown, and we laugh for the reason Kant tells us that we should, 'from the sudden transfiguration of a strained expectation into nothing'. In all of them, tricks of dialect and local colour and an extraordinarily accurate ear for idiom and habitual expression place before us characters whose guileless inadvertence reveals their absurdity in a way that never alienates sympathy. Metaphors are taken literally; what nature has joined is divided for separate inspection, and what in nature was separate is compounded by art; machinery is elaborated to sustain a dream of nonsense in a way that makes the contraptions of Heath Robinson seem ponderous. I shall return to Brian O'Nolan's methods as a writer, and what is important here is to establish the intellectuality

of the laughter *The Best of Myles* provokes. It is not ethical laughter at
human folly, conscious of violations of moral or social or intellectual
propriety: it is instead a laughter that is often not even externalized,
a delight in ingenuity and learning of the same sort associated with
seventeenth-century wit. The element of surprise and invention, the
perception of remote analogies to link the metaphorical and the literal,
the great fertility of knowledge and fecundity of fancy, the parody
and the deflation that magnifies the absurdity of its subject without
destroying it altogether, is like a poem by Cleveland 'Illustrated by
nothing but her self'. The only true comparison for any of the entries
in the Myles na gCopaleen Catechism of Cliché would be a seventeenth-
century satirical poem like *Hudibras*, the short and for ever balanced
question and answer constituting a metre of Isocratic correctness. The
best description of any gCopaleen Research Bureau project is surely as a
conceit which immediately strikes us as more ingenious than possible,
but which aims at making us concede possibility while admiring absurdity.

The quality of humour in *The Best of Myles* is above all witty in the
extent of its remoteness from emotional entanglement. The mimicry
of various voices asks that we recognize them as expressions of various
types of personality—the bore, the railway enthusiast, the legal correspondent—but not that we identify with those personalities in
wholehearted sympathy. And again, the *persona* of Myles is not given
to us as, say, a Parson Adams or a Mr Shandy; its oddities do not call on
our natures but instead sweep us forward with the vigour, the activity
of its productions. It is not a *persona* to draw us in, and though Myles
is occasionally trapped at bus-stops and in bars, he himself pins down the
bores and displays them transfixed. His is not a humour that is turned
in on itself, making fun of itself as of the inefficient bumbling victims
in Thurber; it is never cosy or tinged with self-congratulation, as Paul
Jennings is so often; it does not rest on a sense of social distinctions
and *double entendre* of the English variety, as does so much of Stephen
Potter's humour, and the Dublin and Yeovil Research Bureaux make
an instructive contrast; it is a humour remarkably free from indecency,
ribaldry, or even the mild family recognitions of sexual behaviour one

finds in Ogden Nash. The fact that it is best defined by negatives and negative comparisons is itself significant. Brian O'Nolan's humour in *The Best of Myles* is at its best austere, self-sufficing, pure.

The continuity of *The Best of Myles* with Brian O'Nolan's previously written novels is clear enough. A number of incidental interests are carried across—the odd references to Keats's odes in *At Swim-Two-Birds*, for instance, burgeon into the whole Keats-Chapman syndrome[39]—and the objects of satire and the methods of humour are essentially similar. Thus the birth of the Ringsend cowboys from the horseplay of corner boys and the principle of aestho-autogamy reflects the same habit of the separation of parts and especially the taking of metaphors literally that sustains the various 'runs' of *The Best of Myles*. The curious facts and inaccurate knowledge exchanged by Messrs Furriskey, Lamont and Shanahan (*AS2B*, pp. 273-8) anticipate the serendipity indulged by Myles, and reflect the same mistaken pride and genuine pleasure roused also in MacCruiskeen by the word *bulbul* (*3P*, pp. 65-6, 69).[40] Again and even more obviously, the De Selbean sophistries of *The Third Policeman* are the immediate ancestor of Myles's method: De Selby's speculations on the theory of mirrors, which involve a Zenoistic spatialization of time, are more philosophically oriented but certainly no less bizarre than Myles's comparable suggestions for, say, the ultimate utterly limited edition, so exclusive that 'NO COPY WHATEVER WILL BE PRINTED' (*3P*, pp. 64-5; *BoM*, p. 228); Myles's arguments on the downward house follow the same logic as De Selby on the subject of houses in volume two of his *Golden Hours* (*BoM*, pp. 251-3; *3P*, p. 21).

If, however, *The Best of Myles* continues the De Selbean rhetoric of *The Third Policeman* it does so in an entirely different context, not that of a novel but of a newspaper and not that of a structured argument for which the author is responsible but of a daily column whose purpose is only to divert. The paradoxically more relaxing demand of a newspaper deadline at least at first encouraged the spinning out of fantasy for its own sake. It gave Brian O'Nolan a detachment which allowed him the fiendish stalking of the absurd at its own pace, to press his pursuit of folly into a world of liberated aesthetic activity.

'The young *Cruiskeen Lawn* was like a column that had just left college', remarked Thomas Hogan.[41] Since the framework of the column was given by its surrounding context of serious news and comment, consequences could be ignored and contrivance and invention pursued to a point where their absurdity need not be underscored. Brian O'Nolan's role as newspaperman enabled him to keep a distance from his activity as writer. Though he was serious on occasion, the effect was predominantly to liberate his humour into the pure impersonal activity described. The journalistic *persona* appears to have had the same effect on him as a typewriter has on other writers, enabling them to write outside themselves, and the proportion of allusions to surrounding columns and sheer dissociated doodling within the given space and against the deadline is significantly high. Such dissociation is echoed in the puns which recur in item after item. The following example conveys how Brian O'Nolan's detachment allows him to manipulate freely the mechanism of verbal and human gestures:

I am, of course, intensely interested in education. I have every reason to be because I was disabled for life at the age of fifteen by a zealous master (although I had the laugh on him afterwards when I came back from hospital with my two hands amputated). When I was taking a bath last night (fearful job disconnecting the taps and getting the thing out through the window) I found some bits of paper, blue and gamgee coloured, lying about on the floor. They were examination papers—indeed, they probably still are. . . . [*BoM*, p. 243]

The impersonality of the method hardly needs to be contrasted with the nightmare vision of *The Third Policeman*. It is a witty logic, the sophistry of which the reader has little interest in stopping to quarrel with, for it flatters his love of mischief and makes the sport.

The Best of Myles makes up a very different book again from *At Swim-Two-Birds*, in that *The Third Policeman* has intervened. Its humour is less various and more forceful, centred more on the mechanization of the human and with a touch of asperity, less sweet and wild if also more purely witty.

* * *

An illuminating perspective on the grounds of success of Brian O'Nolan's earlier writing is supplied by the play *Faustus Kelly*, which was staged at the Abbey in January 1943. What is peculiar about the play is the contrast between the first act and the two that follow. The mood of the first is one familiar to readers of *At Swim-Two-Birds* and *The Third Policeman*. The relation between Kelly and the Stranger resembles that between the *Third Policeman*'s narrator and De Selby, in particular, and again the Town Clerk and Shawn resemble Policeman MacCruiskeen and Sergeant Pluck. The dialogue is sheer entertainment and not less so because of the venalities, ambitions and rivalries that sustain it. By contrast, Acts 2 and 3 develop a context for the same petty failings in which they change their hue. The ambition and concupiscence for which Kelly betrays his office—good ambition though it is, and honourable enough affection—magnifies the avariciousness, envy, chauvinism, sectarian feeling over which he must preside. Through his secret fault, good sentiments become ranting:

> As an accredited deputy in the national parliament I am determined to serve my country according to my lights and to the utmost of my talents which God has given me. I am determined to strike blow after blow against the vested interests. I am determined to break— to smash—backstairs jobbery in high places. I am determined to expose—to drag into the inexorable light of day—every knave, time-server, sycophant and party camp-follower. I will meet them all and fight them. [*FK*, p. 97]

Thus the first act, which has all the charm and inconsequence of scenes in *The Third Policeman*'s barracks, is succeeded by two acts in which the moral implications come increasingly to determine how we react to the humour and in fact usurp it. As the contemporary reviewers remarked, 'just as you are convinced that the play is about to get into its proper stride and you sit back to enjoy it, things dawdle into what is almost, but not quite, tediousness'; 'the first act . . . was the funniest thing seen on the stage since *Charley's Aunt* but [it] fizzled out deplorably in the remaining acts.'[42]

Faustus Kelly is paradigmatic of the direction taken by Brian O'Nolan's later writing. Its wit and inventiveness are often the same as before, the remarkable ear and ability to parody a variety of styles are still abundantly evident, but the more conscious moral purpose to which these things are subordinate causes their different effect. Though much of *The Hard Life*, *The Dalkey Archive* and the later 'Cruiskeen Lawn' columns is familiar, where they are successful is altogether different. They are ingenious and convoluted, as before, but also harder, cruder, less fastidious. They are not to be dismissed, as they sometimes are, for being failed versions of what exists better elsewhere for they all possess an undeniable power. What is curious is that as they are dominated by Brian O'Nolan's powerful personality they become less individual to the same extent—less individual, that is, than writing in which one's sense of the author's values had been less clear than one's sense of his detachment, diffidence and even shyness.

The Hard Life is continuous with the previous novels, indeed re-markably so in a number of ways given the twenty-year interval, but it is a book opportunistically written on the wave of renewed con-fidence brought about by the republication of *At Swim-Two-Birds*. It includes motifs developed during the intervening years in 'Cruiskeen Lawn', such as the Brother and the vendetta with that 'gang of ignorant, pot-bellied, sacrilegious, money-scooping robbers, very likely runners from the bogs, hop-off-my-thumbs from God-forsaken places like Carlow or the County Leitrim' (*HL*, p. 83)—that is, Andy Clarkin's Dublin Corporation—but altogether *The Hard Life* is his least successful book. Its relevance here is the new direction it embodies. The title comes from the framing narrative of *At Swim-Two-Birds*—'It is a hard life, but, said Brinsley' (*AS2B*, p. 37)—but what was perceived before with forbearance has become explicitly 'an exegesis of squalor'. At the same time that the narrator of *The Third Policeman* shows his hand as Manus (their dangerous utopian dreams of 'a society in which all *unnecessary* wrongs, failures, and misbehaviours are removed' are almost identical—cf. *3P*, pp. 189–90 and *HL*, p. 102), the 'eye' of the book, linked to him by irrevocable blood ties but disassociated by training and temperament, becomes morally neutral. In this way the book frames a situation, the action involving the characters being merely the way the situation states itself, and one quality of the situation at that. Even so, despite this narrowing and essential simplicity, the tone is uncertain. There is squalor enough, and yet at least one reviewer found it funny, 'a real broth of a book'. We are uncomfortably caught between laughter and pain, and the final proof is the final sentence. Are we prepared, even after more than two hundred pages, for that 'tidal surge of vomit'?

The Dalkey Archive is in all ways a more ambitious book and provides a fairer basis for comparison with the earlier ones. It took Brian O'Nolan a long time to write, it was carefully and completely revised, and he pinned his hopes on its success. It combines all the themes explored in his previous writing and establishes new relations between them in an intellectually more ambitious way. Theology, science and literature are all put to the test and found to be riddled with overweening arrogance, 'the old sin of pride' (*DA*, p. 119). The dedication 'to my Guardian Angel' is likewise not flippant in the company of virgins called Mary, a pub renamed the Colza, of assaults upon the Jesuits and a less than usually ironic exposition of several concerns close to Jansenism. St Augustine's answer is essentially Brian O'Nolan's comment on the ferment he depicts: '*But do you know, I think the greatest dog's breakfast of the lot is St. Vianney.*' (*DA*, p. 40.) The working-out of the theme is contrived with few loose ends or incongruities in a way that reflects the same clarity of purpose. Parallels between characters and incidents are established clearly, links and implications insisted upon with unusual emphasis. The nineteen-year-old literary medical student looking for digs in Dalkey in Chapter 3 (a 'slim, black-haired, callow' no one—*DA*, p. 27) anticipates ominously and anagrammatically the author of the 'intricate and bombastic' *Ulysses* we meet in Skerries, and a variety of means in the later part of the book connect it with the earlier part. Joyce is linked to St Augustine through his own saint's name, of course. His interest in the early Church Fathers follows De Selby's, and his condemnation of the Church for 'inventing' the Holy Spirit follows De Selby's accusation of St Augustine and appropriation for his own use of the D.M.P.; and here we are clearly intended to recall Sergeant Fottrell's intervening disquisition on the central mystery of 'pneumatic bicyclosity'. The later De Selby who experiences a spiritual conversion in this respect merely follows in the wake of Joyce himself, both of them following on the protagonist Mick in their turn.

The position of Mick is close to the author's: he stands at the centre of the book and in him its tensions work themselves out. At times his proximity to the author becomes near downright identification. His list of the tasks confronting him at the opening of Chapter 12 is really Brian O'Nolan's, and his arrangement to meet Hackett at the Westland Row bar is authorially inspired to point up the sort of triviality that obtrudes on the plans of any contriver of plots, however grandiose (cf. *DA*, p. 130). For the same reason, in the course of the book as the plot works itself out, Mick's function is validated and his standing rises. He comes, as he realizes himself, to be a supervisor of men. 'Clearly enough this task had been assigned to him by Almighty God, and this gave him somewhat the status of priest.' (*DA*, p. 156.) Mick's awareness of status before his vocation is none the less a significant priority, and one which makes him at one with De Selby and Joyce; he takes to himself their aims, interpreting them his own way to abandon his mother, his girl, his friends, his job to his self-deluding ambition to become a Cistercian. The parallels between De Selby and Joyce are consequently no more important than the differences as they are made clear in the changed status of Mick on either side of that centrally placed meeting with Sergeant Fottrell. Mick thereafter brings Joyce back to life again, as De Selby had brought back St Augustine and others, and we share his sense of pervasive ambiguity: 'sometimes he seemed to be dictating events with deific authority, at other times he saw himself the plaything of implacable forces' (*DA*, p. 188).

The method is one, familiar from earlier novels, of a play of consciousness within consciousness in a series of enveloping plots—as Coventry Patmore put it in *The Angel in the House*, 'I knew / He thought I thought he thought I slept'—but the differences are more important. Despite the mingling and counterpoint I have described and which underpin the book's themes, it in fact reads as a very much more straightforward narrative than either of its two early predecessors. As against *The Third Policeman*, De Selby is at a conscious level opposed by the central character and this creates a context in which the passages common to the two books have a different effect. The more explicit moral relation that the 'poor man's De Selby'-theorizing of Sergeant Fottrell bears to the rest of the book controls the way we respond to it, which is less as pure humour than also as satire on presumptuous ignorance. Like Mick, we are not taken in by it. The near word-for-word exact duplication of the description of a Strabane landscape in the two books (cf. *3P*, p. 86 and *DA*, p. 89) points up the same difference, for the landscape is less horrifyingly ironic in its second context than a pleasurable relief. We are in one way more certain where we are; and it is a certainty that affects other parts of the book in turn. The satire on the Jesuits is more controlled in its tone than in *The Hard Life*, for example, and extended in its implications. At the same time that the narrator is presented as consciously more well-intentioned, he is also presented as a greater fool. The previous unnamed narrators were given as lazy and apathetic, but the element of derision in the presentation of Mick is stronger even than in the presentation of *The Hard Life*'s Finbarr. A sentence like 'He rather admired his own adroit manipulation of matters which, in certain regards, transcended this world' (*DA*, p. 151), might have described the narrator of *At Swim-Two-Birds* were it not for the cutting edge of complacency observed, which is crucial. Mick's good intentions are all delusions, and his victory less than empty. If we laugh at the end, it is at our own expense and not because we are given something to laugh at. Hugh Leonard's stage adaptation *When the Saints Go Cycling In*, where the D.M.P. is thrown into the sea which is consequently activated, made the derisive attitude towards Mick's mistakes even more certain; but none the less to go this far is to go too far. Just as we are at times surprised by the erratic growth of Mick's developing social concern and opposition to De Selby—his boldness and self-confidence in dealing with Father Cobble at the Royal Marine Hotel and his dispassionately objective appraisal there of De Selby's intellectual and spiritual position (*DA*, p. 119) is startling—so we never settle to a consistent view of him. So, too, though the book contains more explicit aids to understanding its unity than any of the others, it is something less than the sum of its considerable parts.

The derision that accompanies Brian O'Nolan's later more obviously moral humour can be appreciated more exactly by considering his attitude towards Joyce. *At Swim-Two-Birds* makes use of Joyce in the same way as does Raymond Queneau's *On est toujours trop bon avec les femmes* (1947), that is, to an ingeniously bewildering comic purpose. *Dubliners* and *Ulysses* are echoed on a number of occasions, for instance the Circe episode is transposed into a minor key in the trial of Dermot Trellis and the values of the Cyclops citizen reappear in Jem Casey. The use of *A Portrait of the Artist as A Young Man* and *Finnegans Wake* is even more important, and supplies the principle of *At Swim-Two-Birds*'s entire organization. Section V of the *Portrait* becomes the reference point for the verminous dissolute University College student and the *Wake* for his 'work in progress'. The book that Brian O'Nolan's Stephen-figure is writing centres on the dreams of a publican, a 'night-logic' world which obeys its own laws and appears to be liberated from customary physical restraints, all its characters merging into one another around a small core of fixed types. Even the choice of the name Trellis is not without significance when one recalls Joyce's remark to Padraic Colum, 'Of course, I don't take Vico's speculations literally; I use his cycles as a trellis.'[43] The extent to which the use of Joyce controls the organization of *At Swim-Two-Birds* is indicated by the fate of Brinsley. Whereas in fact, as Brian O'Nolan's good friend Niall Sheridan, he is included in the plot as the friend and adviser he was, his role as a Cranly figure overtakes him: he is felt in some way only explicable in terms of the parody to have betrayed the narrator (cf. *AS2B*, pp. 230–5), and so he is rejected.

The uses of Joyce in *At Swim-Two-Birds* are to be set against the attitude of Joyce in the later novels. In the earlier one, the allusions are a level of meaning and one aspect of structure, a way of bringing some order into what is essentially a swirling chiaroscuro of good-humoured fantasy. A moral is implied in the narrator's changed attitude towards his uncle and Mr Corcoran at the end of the book and elsewhere, but only implied. *The Hard Life* and *The Dalkey Archive*, by contrast, invoke Joyce only to degrade him: in the one, it is degradation by allusion to the squalor of Joyce's fictional world in *Dubliners*, the *Portrait* and *Ulysses*[23], from whose contamination the exiled artist-figure Manus is, to say the least, not free; in the other, the critique is more fundamental and more wide-ranging. The implications of Joyce's method are pursued to make plain how it is an expression of universal pride and delusion, and the comment framed by Joyce's fitness only to repair underwear in the laundry is final. Again, what is of interest is not only that the later novels concern themselves with the moral implications of Joyce's aesthetic and example (implications that Brian O'Nolan appears to have made wholly clear to himself in the novel from which Joyce is nominally absent, *The Third Policeman*),[44] but that Brian O'Nolan is very clearly involved and has come to feel for the object of his disapproval all the hatred of a personal vendetta.

The changing attitudes in the novels are confirmed and also extended in the columns of 'Cruiskeen Lawn' and in a number of reviews and essays. These other pieces show the deep impression made on Brian O'Nolan by the enormous growth of Joyce's reputation, particularly in American academic circles. As the Joyce cult grew, his comments became increasingly vituperative. It is as if, while continuing to hold that Joyce was a great writer (even though his art has nothing to do with morality, goodness or beauty), and continuing to defend and to praise him on these grounds, Brian O'Nolan came also, through the seriousness and exhaustiveness of 'the four thousand strong corps of American simpletons now in Dublin doing a thesis on James Joyce' (CL, 9th September, 1949), to find Joyce himself priggish and proud:

> *Finnegans Wake* by reason of language and image left a sort of Wake Island in the sea of literature, yet today it is regarded as a towering *chef d'oeuvre*, used by some people as a prayer book—and indeed I have heard its author referred to as St. James. [CL, 22nd December, 1964]

The growth of Brian O'Nolan's personal animosity in the years between the earlier and later novels can be measured by setting alongside one another his review of Seon Givens's anthology of *Two Decades of Criticism*, which is lightheartedly tongue-in-cheek, with his very much more bitter reaction to Mrs Glasheen's *Census* ten years later (cf. CL, 18th August, 1948 and 20th December, 1957).[45] By the time

Stuart Gilbert had published the first volume of Joyce's letters, Brian O'Nolan had come to see Joyce as 'a complete prig, a snob, and a person possessed of endowment unique in the archives of conceit' (CL, 6th June, 1957).

Brian O'Nolan was always more serious when he wrote about artists in the columns of 'Cruiskeen Lawn', and he was always particularly aware of their reputations (which he usually thought inflated), but what the crucial instance of Joyce indicates are the personal grounds for the increasing loss of poise, the rancorousness, the more sombre tone and occasional malice of his later writing. As Joyce's reputation spread fashionably and profitably across the campuses, it is no wonder that one of the two men of his generation in Ireland fit to be compared with him grew to feel resentment, even persecution. The book on which he was working at the time of his death continues the attack, with an assault on liberal America and its patronage of Ireland, and most would judge it marred by its impulse to degrade. A strain of cruelty is always present in Brian O'Nolan's writing, in the prolonged pains inflicted on Trellis at the end of *At Swim-Two-Birds* or the brutal killing of Mathers in *The Third Policeman*. It is even arguable that there is a degree of malice in the pointlessness of much of the humour of 'Cruiskeen Lawn', that the pleasure derived from the Keats-Chapman jokes is the pleasure of anticipations belittled and that the meticulosity and economy of their way of telling can only be called callous. This is, none the less, a different matter from the pervasively ugly comedy controlling the presentation of Father Fahrt and the death of Collopy in *The Hard Life*, or the grisly blend of murder and taxidermy in the uncollected short story 'Two in One'.[46] Deep disappointments and the unremitting demands of journalism and script-writing put under an intolerable strain a temperament 'which was essentially aristocratic, fastidious and private'.[47]

The shift I have described is at its worst from detachment to intolerance, at its best from fastidiousness to what Brian O'Nolan himself called 'scorpiousness'. If the later writing is sometimes tired or savage, the earlier writing is occasionally tedious in its profusion and pointlessness, but in each case such falling-off is inevitable and the conditions of success and failure are in each case the same. The difference between Brian O'Nolan's early and late writing, his worst and his best, is less a difference of manner than a different use to which the manner is put. A framework of ordinary values preserves the purity of the fantasy in both a novel like *At Swim-Two-Birds* and the collection *The Best of Myles*, and a more conscious apprehension of the same framework makes the later journalism more sombre, but the manner which is framed and which produces the different effect is itself remarkably consistent. Shawn and the Town Clerk in *Faustus Kelly* do not talk very differently in Acts 2 and 3 from the way they talk in Act 1, and in this, as in other ways as I have said, the play is paradigmatic.

The framework of Brian O'Nolan's writing changes to control the degree and kind of distance between himself as man and himself as writer, but always man and writer appear to have needed this common condition of distance. This is the controlling feature of all aspects of his style. The way in which he characteristically found inspiration in less obvious and more commonplace sources, approaching the ordinary in a quite unordinary way, is connected to his ability to set apart or frame phrases which are intrinsically gratuitous but thereby are given an indestructible permanence; Lamont's account of Sergeant Craddock and the lucubrations of the Plain People of Ireland are examples from *At Swim-Two-Birds*. Brian O'Nolan's economic, precise, even surgical control of language gives a flavour of salt to his writing and preserves it from the dullness and banality it so often caricatures; he holds words at a distance, aware of their misuse and the incongruities they conceal. The puns of 'Cruiskeen Lawn' are less a fusion of meanings than a dispassionate separation of them to reveal their antithetical absurdity. 'Ever do the History of Rome by 54y at school? Sorry—I mean Livy.' (*BoM*, pp. 257-8.) The conclusion of a representative Keats-Chapman dialogue does not grow out of what builds up to it but ostentatiously turns its back on the setting, using it only to silhouette the opposition between sound and sense or as an echo-box for the blank cartridge to resound more hollowly. The same dissociation is reflected in the terseness with which the words are put together. Brian O'Nolan is not happy in long sentences, which progress cautiously with the forms of subordination and connection clearly expressed, characteristically substituting clipped emphatic pronouns like *he* and *it* for *who* and *which*. The sentences are usually short and their elegance concise and antithetical. There is little more connection between the short sharp questions and answers of the Myles na gCopaleen Catechism of Cliché than between the sentences of one of Bacon's early essays; and against the success of Brian O'Nolan's parodies of *Time* (e.g. *BoM*, p. 89), it is noticeable that he forgoes opportunities to attempt the cadenced, evolving elegance of a writer like Proust (whom he instead more successfully assails through certain of Proust's readers—e.g. *BoM*, p. 113). Another notable illustration of the same feature is the series in 'Cruiskeen Lawn' of dialogues at the bus-stop concerning the Brother. As phobically single-minded monologues which only develop with the refrain-like interjections of the pinned auditor, they change direction not within any one sentence or group of sentences but instead between the groups of sentences, or, as it were, stanzas. The sentences have little drama of their own, and the largest part of their unpredictable life and the whole possibility of their moving forward lies in these punctuations of comic relief. Or again there is the example of *The Third Policeman* in relation to *À Rebours*. When so much of the book's manner is identical with that of Huysmans', from the peculiar isolated quality of the chapters, to the fetishistic concern with authorities and a tradition of the perverse, to a concern with technical and especially mechanical contrivance, the contrast at the level of style is the more obvious. Brian O'Nolan is uniformly at a much greater distance from the subject he treats. Huysmans' colourful, complex, decadent style gives way to one that is droll, less tiring, almost brisk.

The broad relevance of Brian O'Nolan's background as a native Irish speaker to his English style is the same. It is doubtless possible to show that this or that verbal and grammatical habit derives from the Irish, just as it is possible to situate his writing in general centrally in a native Irish tradition,[48] but it is more relevant and certainly less controversial to accept the native Irish tradition in the way he himself suggested as something utterly gratuitous, a world quite apart: 'it attracts even by its surpassing difficulty, for scarcely anybody living today can write or speak Irish correctly and exactly in the fashion of 300 years ago' (*BoM*, p. 282). His attitude to fashionable attempts to link language directly with politics is written out at large in *An Béal Bocht*. He had little sympathy with efforts to establish a Gaelic-speaking potato-digging republic, pinned together with bicycle clips and handball medals. What his Irish gave him was not some mysterious folk myth or compulsion to follow in a shanachie tradition of popular anecdote and histrionic humour, but an ability to preserve a stance outside the element he more commonly moved in, a sense of detachment from it. The quality he praises as a feature of Irish writing is significantly not its abandon but the reverse, its 'steely latinistic' quality and 'complete precision in the use of words' (*BoM*, pp. 282–3), which is particularly significant if one recalls the at times extraordinarily convoluted almost baroque inversions and ornaments of his own Irish style. 'Pisa bec oc Parnabus'[49] is a special case, being a straightforward imitation-parody of the texture of Joyce's *Work in Progress*, but there is nothing quite like it in his English writing. The qualities Brian O'Nolan praises are in fact more clearly transmitted in his English verse translations from the Irish and, more pervasively if less directly, in the exactitude of his own original English style. His detachment from 'H.M. English' (*BoM*, p. 351) gives him the ability to dismantle and reassemble it like a machine, abets his awareness of *cliché* and revulsion from slovenliness: 'I often wonder am I . . . mad? Do I take that rather Irish thing, O'Fence, too easily? I go into a house, for instance. My "host" says "sit down". Now why *down*? Why must he be so cautious and explicit. . . .' (*BoM*, p. 361.)

Brian O'Nolan's bilingualism, from the point of view of his writing in English, only emphasized and extended in it a quality that was anyway central. His wit, for instance, depends very much on the controlled perception of item after item, just as so much of his ingenuity focuses on the giving of separate attention to parts of a process which in reality can only be continuous: the similar observation of the moving roll of fat on the uncle's neck in *At Swim-Two-Birds* and on Sergeant Pluck's neck in *The Third Policeman* (*AS2B*, p. 133 and *3P*, p. 120) are examples, as are the inventions of De Selby and MacCruiskeen, or even the Brother's theorizing on the egg that never dies (*BoM*, p. 52) and Myles's calamitously literal understanding of 'keeping your eyes skinned' ('I admit the skin *does* grow rather quickly, but what are surgeons for?' (*BoM*, p. 292)). The same detachment is evident in Brian O'Nolan's descriptions and his dialogue. Landscapes are seen as stilled pictures possessed of a surface shimmer, given life by the intrusion of an unlooked for detail. Controlling the way we respond to what is recognizably the countryside round Strabane or Dalkey-Killiney is an undisguised contrivance, and the air of flaunted theatricality ('as if a curtain had been miraculously whisked away' (*DA*, p. 7)) is part of their charm. Art is employed not to create what Baudelaire called 'une déformation sublime de la nature', but to contain, to qualify, almost to decreate. Dialogue likewise gives little sense of the real interplay of minds reaching out and finding each other dramatically in words; the pressure of complicating human involvement beneath the simple surfaces is absent. All the dialogue does is to juxtapose surfaces, the alternation of speakers being in effect a means of etching their outlines more clearly but not of filling them in or rounding them out. 'Mr. De Selby, Hackett said with a want of gravity, would it be rude to ask just how you will destroy the world? You did not make it.' (*DA*, p. 19.) Brian O'Nolan's handling of narrative is noticeably by way of such set scenes and formally projected encounters. The story interest of all the books is slight, as is our continuous identification with the characters involved. Since the construction of his novels tends to be episodic, the artificial limits of the 'Cruiskeen Lawn' column were not so inhibiting as they might have been to a writer of a different sort; he was able to do 'runs' or sequences centering on some common anecdote or in a shared manner, and all his larger constructions exist only to relate to one another a variety of shorter more or less self-sufficient pieces of writing. Brian O'Nolan rightly felt more at ease with three plots than with one, *The Hard Life* being the least counter-pointed and least successful of the novels. It is a noticeable feature of uncollected short stories like 'The Martyr's Crown' and 'Donabate'[50] that they are recognizably scenes from unwritten novels, and yet, because they lack that larger relation, their effect is much diminished.

In the same way, new readers of *The Best of Myles* volume need to establish a context, to read a number of pages, before any one page of Myles's wit begins to work on them. Brian O'Nolan did not find the relating of parts to one another easy—it took some time to achieve in the case of *At Swim-Two-Birds* (and even then his solution is partly to parade his deficiencies so as to point up the inconsequence of the models parodied), and the relative, painlessly achieved, coherence of *The Third Policeman* misled him to think the plot was the 'only good thing about it' (cf. *3P*, p. 200)—but these relations define how we come at any one of the parts taken singly and determine their effect.

The continuous characteristics of Brian O'Nolan's method as a writer all serve to keep us at a slight distance from the material, from what Wordsworth was aware of as 'Reality too close and too intense'. This is the burden of the rule that the strongest influences on him were those he worked against most strongly. The only large exception to the rule is the native Irish tradition, but the way he conceived this as a world apart thereby connects such characteristics with his preference always to write in the guise of a *persona*. Only the translations of the Čapeks' *Insect Play* and Brinsley MacNamara's *Mairéad Gillan*[51] were done in his own name; and he maintained that, 'for the purpose of literary utterance', 'the compartmentation of [the writer's] personality . . . ensures that the fundamental individual will not be credited with a certain way of thinking, fixed attitudes, irreversible techniques of expression'.[52] As Mary puts it in *The Dalkey Archive*, 'One must write outside oneself. I'm fed up with writers who put a fictional gloss over their own squabbles and troubles.' (*DA*, p. 221.) The claim is at least as significant as the accomplishment, and ultimately more so. Matt Duffy, John James Doe and George Knowall for a start can be dismissed as pale reflections of the pressures of syndicated journalism, which leaves Brother Barnabas, Flann O'Brien and Myles na gCopaleen.

Whatever Brian O'Nolan would prefer us to believe, he does not assume a new style with each *persona* and each *persona* itself presides over a range of styles. Myles na gCopaleen is not properly a *persona* at all, being manifestly little more in origin than an appropriate expedient suggested by the invitation to write for the *Irish Times*. It gave him the licence of peasant jester before a readership which, in the early forties, was very different from what it is now and such that Cumann Liteardha na Gaedhilge of U.C.D. solemnly passed a motion congratulating the paper on publishing its new Irish column.[53] The pseudonym was continued not only as the column declined into English but beyond it to *Faustus Kelly* on the one hand, to *An Béal Bocht* on the other, and to a variety of shorter pieces. The *persona* of Flann O'Brien is a similarly accidentally-derived pseudonym. Once assumed for that metaphorical flan of Brian O'Nolan, *At Swim-Two-Birds*, its continuity is stretched beyond credible limit in the much more tightly organized *Third Policeman* and the otherwise very different *Hard Life* and *Dalkey Archive*. Again, it would not be possible to attribute to either *persona* on internal grounds of subject, style or attitude the uncollected stories, essays and reviews scattered through *The Bell*, *Irish Writing*, *Envoy* and the rest. What distinguishes 'The Trade in Dublin' from 'Drink and Time in Dublin', or 'The Dance Halls' from 'Pots and Pains'?[54] Only the fact that in later years he preferred to be thought of as Myles.

Brian O'Nolan's style is considerably less varied than that of many other writers who have not adopted *personae*, for instance Coleridge's, and a comparison with a writer like Swift makes plain that each *persona* effects not so much a change of style as an initial change of context for that style, marking a changed degree of control over it which alters its effect. Brother Barnabas from Brian O'Nolan's undergraduate years presided over (if that is the phrase) a world of delirious fantasy, and gave way to the two others which indicate the different conditions under which he came to feel he was writing and under which his own personality could find oblique but unambiguous and developing expression. As should be clear by now, when the sense of control increased in the novels the journalism had also become more sombre, and the centre of attraction in each had changed.

Brian O'Nolan characteristically needed a *persona* of some sort to liberate him into the full exploitation of his gifts. The way in which he resisted all attempts to invade his privacy, as he did all manner of

pretension and egocentricity, is very noticeable in *The Best of Myles*.
He does not want to be told how to think by examiners in literature,
or by pundits on modern painting, or by *aficionados* of the cinema, or
by the supporters of such (then) fashionable crusades as that against the
Censorship Board and, differently, on behalf of the G.A.A.: 'These
people, disdaining extraordinary water, call themselves "Common
Ground". With gigantic presumption they begin by calling me "Dear
Sir".' (*BoM*, p. 254.) Equally revealing is his understanding of the
novel as a thing to be 'self-administered in private' (*AS2B*, p. 32), and
his acclamation of an *oeuvre* to be described as 'a . . . sort of legendary
organism which is to be appreciated and can only be judged in terms
of itself' (*BoM*, p. 260)—the tongue-in-cheek tone here being a necessary condition of the succinctness. The student in *At Swim-Two-Birds*
has a father, though we may easily forget it, and Mick in *The Dalkey
Archive* his mother, but characteristically Brian O'Nolan's protagonists
are orphaned and alone. The area in Brian O'Nolan's mind where the
many contradictory elements came together at a distance from his
writing is private and apart. What one feels to be its least disguised
and uncomplicated expression, such as the poems from the Irish in *At
Swim-Two-Birds* or the others still uncollected, is spare, perfect and
unyielding:

> My hand has a pain from writing,
> Not steady the sharp tool of my craft
> Its slender beak spews bright ink—
> A beetle-dark shining draught.
>
> Streams of wisdom of white God
> From my fair-brown, fine hand sally,
> On the page they splash their flood
> In ink of the green-skinned holly.
>
> My little dribbly pen stretches
> Across the great white paper plain,
> Insatiable for splendid riches—
> That is why my hand has a pain![55]

Notes

1. In 'Recent Irish Poetry', *The Bookman*, LXXXVI, August 1934, pp. 235–6, under the pseudonym of 'Andrew Belis'.
2. As Mervyn Wall put it in his review of *The Best of Myles* ('Mylestones'), *Irish Times*, 14th September, 1968, p. 8.
3. References to Brian O'Nolan's books are given thus in the text, the page number following the abbreviated title in the bracketed reference. The following abbreviations are employed: *AS2B* for *At Swim-Two-Birds* (London: Longmans 1939 and MacGibbon & Kee 1960); *FK* for *Faustus Kelly* (Dublin: Cahill 1943); *HL* for *The Hard Life* (London: MacGibbon & Kee 1961); *DA* for *The Dalkey Archive* (London: MacGibbon & Kee 1964); *3P* for *The Third Policeman* (London: MacGibbon & Kee 1967); *BoM* for *The Best of Myles* (London: MacGibbon & Kee 1968). References to uncollected 'Cruiskeen Lawn' columns in the *Irish Times* are given as CL together with the date. References to Brian O'Nolan's other periodical writings are given in full in the notes.
4. Cf. Niall Sheridan, 'Brian, Flann and Myles', *Irish Times*, 1st April, 1971, p. 10.
5. 'A Bash in the Tunnel', *Envoy*, V, April 1951, p. 11.
6. Review of L. A. G. Strong's *The Sacred River* in *Irish Writing*, No. 10, January 1950, p. 72.
7. Mervyn Wall's phrase is an interview with Michael Smith included in *The Lace Curtain*, No. 4, summer 1971, p. 81.
8. *Loc. cit.*, p. 82.
9. *Point Counter Point*, Chatto & Windus, London 1928, ch. 26, p. 439. Huxley here echoes Arnold in the 'Porro Unum Est Necessarium' chapter of *Culture and Anarchy*: yet another way to describe Brian O'Nolan's position is as a similarly subtle blend of Hellenism and Hebraism.
10. 'Baudelaire and Kavanagh', *Envoy*, III, November 1950, pp. 80, 79.
11. Letter from S. Beckett to J. Knowlson, 8 January 1971, quoted in James Knowlson (ed.), *Samuel Beckett: An Exhibition*, Turret Books, London 1971, p. 29.

12. Interview with Israel Schenker, 'Moody Man of Letters', *New York Times*, 6th May, 1956, section 2, p. 1.
13. *Proust*, Chatto & Windus, London 1931, pp. 16–17.
14. *Murphy*, Routledge, London 1938, ch. 6, p. 112.
15. 'An Aristophanic Sorcerer', *Irish Times*, 2nd April, 1966, p. 7.
16. John Wain, 'To Write for My Own Race', *Encounter*, XXIX, July 1967 p. 80.
17. Niall Montgomery's description in the course of his discussion of Beckett, 'No Symbols Where None Intended', *New World Writing*, No. 5, April 1954, p. 326.
18. Cf. his memorial appreciation, 'Standish Hayes O'Grady', *Irish Times*, 16th October, 1940, p. 3.
19. Brian O'Nolan's attention was undoubtedly drawn to it by its place illustrating Philip Quarles's thoughts on the novel, which bear on *At Swim-Two-Birds*: cf. *Point Counter Point*, ch. 22 (*ed. cit.*, p. 409).
20. Cf. the quotations assembled by Marvin Magalaner and Richard M. Kain in *Joyce: The Man, the Work, the Reputation*, New York University Press, New York 1956, pp. 209–10, 280.
21. In 'James Joyce', *The Catholic World*, CXXXII, March 1931, pp. 641–52: cited by Magalaner and Kain, *op. cit.*, p. 189.
22. *Ulysses on the Liffey*, Faber & Faber, London 1972, p. 36.
23. Allusions to the first two books are obvious. For the last, Mr Collopy's life-long project takes off from a thought of Bloom's in *Lestrygonians* that there 'Ought to be places for women', etc.
24. Niall Sheridan's phrase in the course of a review in *Ireland Today*, II, November 1937, p. 88.
25. Like John Coleman ('The Uses of Joyce') in *The Spectator*, CCV, 22nd July, 1960, p. 141.
26. As has been done by A. A. Mendilow in *Time and the Novel*, Peter Nevill, London 1952, pp. 224–8 esp.
27. *The Field of Nonsense*, Chatto & Windus, London, 1952.
28. 'Brian, Flann and Myles', *Irish Times*, 1st April, 1971, p. 10.
29. Possibly an allusion to triadic motifs in Joyce, possibly to the triadic logic of the Nolan himself (Giordano Bruno).
30. 'An Aristophanic Sorcerer', *Irish Times*, 2nd April, 1966, p. 7.
31. In his review of *At Swim-Two-Birds* ('Secret Scripture'), *Irish Times*, 30th July, 1960, p. 6.
32. Or with the English translations by J. G. O'Keefe also included in his edition of *Buile Suibhne*, Irish Texts Society, XII, David Nutt, London 1913. Cf. *AS2B*, pp. 91–2 with *ed. cit.*, pp. 12 and 13, for instance, or *AS2B*, pp. 124–5 with *ed. cit.*, pp. 136 and 137.

33. 'Scel Lem Duib', *The Lace Curtain*, No. 4, summer 1971, p. 47. For versions of the lay that Sweeny sang, cf. *Buile Suibhne*, ed. cit., pp. 33 and 35; John Montague, 'Sweetness (from the Irish). I. M. Flann O'Brien, who skipped it', *A Chosen Light*, MacGibbon & Kee, London 1967, p. 65.

34. Cf. *3P*, pp. 32–3 and J.-K. Huysmans, *À Rebours* (1884), ch. I, Fasquelle, Paris 1970, pp. 39–41.

35. Cf. *3P*, pp. 50–2 and *À Rebours*, ch. II, ed. cit., pp. 47–51.

36. Cf. *3P*, pp. 106–11 and *À Rebours*, ch. IV, ed. cit., pp. 77–9.

37. Cf. *3P*, pp. 144–8 and *À Rebours*, ch. IX, ed. cit., pp. 136–7.

38. Cf. *À Rebours*, ch. IV, ed. cit., pp. 79–82. Brian O'Nolan doubtless also had Joyce in mind, who complained that in his forties he had a head filled with decaying ambitions and a mouth filled with rotting teeth.

39. The Keats theme extends into *The Hard Life*, with Collopy's death in Rome and his epitaph (*HL*, p. 150). Had Brian O'Nolan fixed on Keats's priorities concerning Beauty and Truth?

40. MacCruiskeen's curious insistence on the word possibly picks up the 'grillon enfermé' of *À Rebours*, ch. I, ed. cit., p. 38, possibly the Keatsian theme of 'Darkling he listened' from *AS2B*, p. 292. Cf. also 'I could hear a morning wind making its way indomitably throughout the world and all the low unsilence of the daytime was in my ear, bright and restless like a caged bird', *3P*, p. 120; etc.

41. 'Myles na gCopaleen', *The Bell*, XIII, November 1946, p. 131.

42. Richard Watts, 'Guest Critic', *The Bell*, V, March 1943, p. 484; Thomas Hogan, op. cit., p. 130.

43. Though the comment was not published, as far as I know, until twenty years after *At Swim-Two-Birds*: cf. Mary and Padraic Colum, *Our Friend James Joyce*, Heinemann, London 1959, p. 123.

44. Various connections of course exist. De Selby echoes Joyce in demanding that his readers should devote their whole lives to reading his works; his cogitations on the house as box recall Joyce's epigram in the 'Hades' chapter of *Ulysses* that 'the Irishman's house is his coffin'. The relevance to Joyce's handling of time of the lucubrations of J. W. Dunne and of Einsteinian physics, which admittedly were in Brian O'Nolan's mind when he wrote *The Third Policeman*, was clear to many commentators in the 1930's and is glossed by Clive Hart, *Structure and Motif in 'Finnegans Wake'*, Faber & Faber, London 1962, pp. 64f., 93f., etc.

45. Or by consulting David Powell, 'An Annotated Bibliography of Myles na Gopaleen's (Flann O'Brien's) "Cruiskeen Lawn" Commentaries on James Joyce', *James Joyce Quarterly*, IX, fall 1971, pp. 50–62—from which the references in this paragraph have been taken.

46. *The Bell*, XIX, July 1954, pp. 30–4.

47. Niall Sheridan's judgment: 'Brian, Flann and Myles', *Irish Times*, 1st April, 1971, p. 10.
48. As is attempted by Benedict Kiely, *Modern Irish Fiction—A Critique*, Golden Eagle Books, Dublin 1950, pp. 74–7, etc.; and Vivian Mercier, *The Irish Comic Tradition*, Clarendon Press, Oxford 1962, pp. 38–40, 104, etc.
49. *Ireland Today*, III, February 1938, pp. 138, 165.
50. In *Envoy*, I, February 1950, pp. 57–62; and *Irish Writing*, Nos 20–1, November 1952, pp. 41–2, respectively.
51. And a few stray pieces such as 'Pisa bec oc Parnabus' and 'The Martyr's Crown' (both already cited), or published posthumously (like 'After Hours', *Threshold*, No. 21, summer 1967, pp. 15–18).
52. 'Do Me', *New Ireland* (magazine of the New Ireland Society of Queen's University, Belfast), March 1964, pp. 41–2.
53. *Irish Times*, 30th October, 1940, p. 6.
54. Flann O'Brien, 'The Trade in Dublin', *The Bell*, I, October 1940, pp. 19–24; Myles na gCopaleen, 'Drink and Time in Dublin', *Irish Writing*, No. 1, 1946, pp. 71–7; Flann O'Brien, 'The Dance Halls', *The Bell*, I, February 1941, pp. 44–52; Myles na gCopaleen, 'Pots and Pains', *The Irish Housewife*, 1963–4, pp. 70–1.
55. 'The Tired Scribe (from the Irish)', *Poetry Ireland*, No. 4, January 1949, p. 12.

Sweetness (from the Irish)

I. M. FLANN O'BRIEN, WHO SKIPPED IT
So Sweeney flew on until he reached the church of Swim Two Birds, opposite Clonmacnoise. He landed on a Friday, to be exact; the clerics were chanting Nones while women beat flax and one was giving birth. As he watched from his tree, Sweeney heard the Vesper bell ring and felt compelled to this poem:

> Although my claws weaken
> Sweeter across water
> The cuckoo's soft call
> Than girn of church-bell.
>
> Woman, don't give birth,
> Nevertheless, on a Friday,
> When even Mad King Sweeney
> Fasts for the King of Truth.
>
> As the women scutch flax—
> Though I say it myself—
> So were my folk scutched
> At the battle of Mag Rath.
>
> From Loch Diolar of the cliffs
> To Derry Colm Cille
> It wasn't war I heard
> From melodious, proud swans.

SWEETNESS (FROM THE IRISH)

And the belling of the stag
In Siodhmhuine's steep glen;
No music on earth soothes
My soul like its sweetness.

O hear me, Christ
Without stain, never
Let me be severed
Oh Christ, from your sweetness!

JOHN MONTAGUE

Bibliographical Notes

IT is premature to attempt a full bibliography of Brian O'Nolan's work. He took many pseudonyms, not all of which have yet been properly accounted for. His contributions to *Comhthrom Féinne* (principally under the name of 'Brother Barnabas') and to *Blather* require further elucidation, while his contributions to the *Sunday Review*, the *Southern Star* (Skibbereen) or the *Nationalist and Leinster Times* (Carlow) are better pursued on another occasion than this.

The largest collection of material relating to his literary activities exists in the Rare Book Room of Morris Library, Southern Illinois University, Carbondale, Illinois. Typescripts of all his published novels (except *At Swim-Two-Birds*, which is in the University of Texas) are held there, his correspondence between 1938 and 1966, together with many articles, reviews and columns under his own name(s) and the pseudonyms. Southern Illinois also holds a typescript of an unfinished novel, *Slattery's Sago Saga* (known otherwise as *The Great Sago Saga*).

In preparing the following selected list of books and writings by and about Brian O'Nolan, I have been much indebted to Mr Michael Hewson of the National Library in Dublin, to Mr David Powell of Western New Mexico University and to Mr J. C. C. Mays of University College, Dublin.

T.O'K.

A: BOOKS BY BRIAN O'NOLAN

1. *At Swim-Two-Birds.* By Flann O'Brien. Longmans, Green, London 1939.

    (Pantheon, New York 1939; MacGibbon & Kee, London 1960; Walker, New York 1966.)

    Reprint editions: Four Square Books, London 1962; Penguin Books, Modern Classics, London 1967; Viking Press, Compass Books, New York 1967.

    In translation as: *Kermesse Irlandaise* (translated by Henri Morisset), Gallimard, Paris 1964; *Zwei Vögel beim Schwimmen* (translated by Lore Fiedler), Rowohlt, Hamburg 1966; *Una pinta d'inchiostro irlandese* (translated by Rodolfo J. Wilcock), Einaudi, Turin 1968.

2. *An Béal Bocht nó an Milléanach: Droch-sgéal ar an droch-shaoghal curtha i n-eagar* le Myles na gCopaleen. An Preas Náisiúnta, Áth Cliath [1941].

    (An treas eagar, Cló Dolmen, Áth Cliath 1964.)

3. *Cruiskeen Lawn.* By Myles na gCopaleen (selection from the columns in the *Irish Times*). Cahill, Dublin [1943].

4. *Faustus Kelly* (a play in three acts). By Myles na gCopaleen. Cahill, Dublin 1943.

5. *Mairéad Gillan.* (A translation into Irish of *Margaret Gillan* by Brinsley MacNamara.) Stationery Office, Dublin 1953.

6. *The Hard Life: An Exegesis of Squalor.* By Flann O'Brien. MacGibbon & Kee, London 1962.

    (Pantheon, New York 1962.)

    Reprint edition: Four Square Books, London 1964.

    In translation as: *Das Harte Leben* (translated by Annemarie and Heinrich Böll and illustrated by Patrick Swift), Nannen, Hamburg 1966; *De Whiskywezen* (translated by M. Marshall-van Wieringen), Meulenhoff, Amsterdam 1970; *Une Vie de Chien* (translated by Christiane Convers), Gallimard, Paris 1972.

7. *The Dalkey Archive.* By Flann O'Brien. MacGibbon & Kee, London 1964.

    (Macmillan, New York 1965.)

8. *The Third Policeman.* By Flann O'Brien. MacGibbon & Kee, London 1967. [Posthumous.]
(Walker, New York 1967.)
Reprint edition: Lancer Books, New York 1970.
In translation as: *Il terzo poliziotto* (translated by Bruno Fonzi), Einaudi, Turin 1971; *De Derde Politieman* (translated by Caspar Hendriks), Bruna, Utrecht 1971.

9. *The Best of Myles.* By Myles na Gopaleen (Flann O'Brien). A selection from 'Cruiskeen Lawn'. Edited and with a Preface by Kevin O Nolan. MacGibbon & Kee, London 1968. [Posthumous.]
(Walker, New York 1968.)

B: Contributions to Books and Periodicals
(As Brian O'Nolan, Brian Nolan, Myles na gCopaleen/Gopaleen, Flann O'Brien)

1. Contributions to *Comhthrom Féinne* (later *The National Student*), published for the Students' Representative Council, University College, Dublin.
Volume I, number 1 appeared on 1st May, 1931. Brian O'Nolan's contributions, which are sometimes serious and more often not, in verse and in prose, English and Irish, extend over the following years. They appear over his own name or over his initials, but more frequently under such pseudonyms as Brother Barnabas or anonymously. [BO'N, variously.]

2. *Blather* ('The Only Paper Exclusively Devoted to the interests of Clay-Pigeon Shooting in Ireland'; 'The Only Really Nice Paper Circulating in Ireland'; etc.) Volume I, Nos 1–5 (all published), August 1934–January 1935. [BO'N, largely.]

3. 'Pisa bec oc Parnabus: Extractum O Bhark l bPragrais', *Ireland Today*, February 1938, Vol. III, No. 2, pp. 138, 165. BO'N.

4. 'Standish Hayes O'Grady', *Irish Times*, 16th October, 1940. FO'B.

5. 'Going to the Dogs! A Discourse on Greyhound Racing in Dublin', *The Bell*, October 1940, Vol. 1, No. 1, pp. 19–24. FO'B.

6. 'Cruiskeen Lawn', *Irish Times*, 4th October, 1940 to 1st April, 1966. MnagC/MnaG. (Sections reprinted in *nonplus*, Nos 1–4, October 1959 to winter 1960. MnagC.

7. 'The Trade in Dublin', *The Bell*, November 1940, Vol. I, No. 2, pp. 6–15. FO'B.

8. 'The Dance Halls', *The Bell*, February 1941, Vol. 1, No. 5, pp. 44–52. FO'B.

9. 'John Duffy's Brother', *Story*, July to August 1941, pp. 65–8. FO'B.

10. 'Drink and Time in Dublin', *Irish Writing*, No. 1, 1946, pp. 71–7. MnagC. (Reprinted in *1000 Years of Irish Prose*, ed. Vivian Mercier and David H. Greene, Devin-Adair, New York 1952, pp. 509–15.)

11. 'The Tired Scribe: a poem from the Irish', *Poetry Ireland*, No. 4, January 1949, p. 12. MnaG.

12. Review of L. A. G. Strong: *The Sacred River: An Approach to James Joyce*; *Irish Writing*, No. 10, January 1950, pp. 71–2. MnagC.

13. 'The Martyr's Crown', *Envoy*, Vol. 1, February 1950, No. 3, pp. 57–62. BN.
   (Reprinted in *Irish Stories and Tales*, ed. Devin A. Garrity, Washington Square Press, New York 1961, pp. 216–21.)
   In translation as: 'De martelaars kroon' (translated by Rolf Loeber) in *Moderne Ierse verhalen*, Polak & Van Gennep, Amsterdam 1967, pp. 82–7.

14. Review of Patrick Campbell: *A Long Drink of Cold Water*; *Irish Writing*, No. 11, May 1950, p. 73. MnaG.

15. 'Baudelaire and Kavanagh', *Envoy*, Vol. III, No. 12, November 1950, pp. 78–81. MnaG.

16. 'A Bash in the Tunnel' (concerning James Joyce), *Envoy*, Vol. V, No. 17, April 1951, pp. 5–11. BN.
   (Reprinted in *A Bash in the Tunnel* ed. John Ryan, Clifton Books, Paignton 1970, pp. 15–20.)

17. 'I don't know', *Kavanagh's Weekly*, Vol. I, No. 3, 26th April, 1952, p. 3. MnaG.

18. 'The New "Phoenix"', *Kavanagh's Weekly*, Vol. I, No. 4, 3rd May, 1952, p. 4. MnaG.

19. 'How are you off for Tostals?', *Kavanagh's Weekly*, Vol. I, No. 5, 10th May, 1952, p. 4. MnaG.

20. Letter to Editor, *Kavanagh's Weekly*, Vol. I, No. 6, 17th May, 1952, p. 5. MnaG.

21. 'Motor Economics', *Kavanagh's Weekly*, Vol. I, No. 7, 24th May, 1952, p. 6. MnaG.

22. Letter to Editor, *Kavanagh's Weekly*, Vol. I, No. 10, 14th June, 1952, p. 5. MnaG.

23. 'Donabate: A Story', *Irish Writing*, Nos 20–1, November 1952, pp. 41–2. MnaG.

24. 'Mad Sweeny *versus* Jem Casey' (extract from *At Swim-Two-Birds*), *1000 Years of Irish Prose*, ed. Vivian Mercier and David H. Greene, Devin-Adair, New York 1952, pp. 563–82. FO'B.

25. 'Two in One: A Story', *The Bell*, Vol. XIX, No. 8, July 1954, pp. 30–4. MnaG.

26. Notes on U.C.D. and the Literary and Historical Society, *Centenary History of the Literary and Historical Society 1855–1955*, ed. James Meenan, The Kerryman Ltd., Tralee, undated, pp. 240–6. BO'N.

27. 'Words', *Development: The Journal of Ireland's Economic Recovery*, Spring Show, 1959, p. 1. FO'B.

28. 'National Gallery: Sean O'Sullivan', *Development*, December 1959, p. 1. FO'B.

29. 'Public Taste and Decorum', *Hibernia*, XXIV, 9th September, 1960, p. 3. MnaG.

30. 'Small Men and Black Dogs', *Manchester Guardian*, 14th October, 1960. BN.

31. 'Christmas Time at Santry', *The Harp*, December 1960, Vol. III, No. 6, p. 8. MnaG.

32. 'This Job of Work', *Evening Mail*, 12th October, 1961. MnaG.

33. 'Myles, By an Admirer', *The Harp*, Vol. IV, No. 5, December 1961, p. 19. [Anonymous.]

34. 'Old Hat Re-Blocked', *Irish Times*, 14th March, 1962. FO'B.

35. 'Enigma', *Irish Times*, 16th June, 1962. FO'B.
36. 'The Fausticity of Kelly', *Radio-TV Guide*, 23rd January, 1963. MnaG.
37. 'Pots and Pains', *The Irish Housewife*, XIV (1963-4), pp. 70-1. MnaG.
38. 'Behan, Master of Language', *Sunday Telegraph*, 22nd March, 1964. FO'B.
39. 'Do Me', *New Ireland*, March 1964, pp. 41-2. MnaG.
40. 'Gael Days', *Manchester Guardian*, 6th May, 1964. FO'B.
41. 'St Augustine Strikes Back: De scribendi periculo', *Bookmark* (World Book Fair Special), 1964, p. 2. FO'B.
42. 'A Man and his Bicycle' (pre-publication extract from *The Dalkey Archive*), *Queen*, 13th August, 1964, pp. 46-9. FO'B.
43. 'George Bernard Shaw on Language', *Irish Times*, 23rd January, 1965. FO'B.
44. 'At the Crossroads', *Irish Times*, 20th February, 1965. FO'B.
45. 'A Pint of Plain' (reprinted from *At Swim-Two-Birds*), *The Harp*, summer 1965, Vol. VIII, No. 2, p. 27. MnaG.
46. 'The Cud of Memory', *Manchester Guardian*, 15th October, 1965. FO'B.
47. 'Can a Saint Hit Back?' *Manchester Guardian*, 19th January, 1966. FO'B.
48. 'A Christmas Garland', *The Harp*, Christmas 1966, Vol. IX, No. 4, p. 19. MnaG.
49. 'After Hours: A Short Story', *Threshold*, summer 1967, No. 21, pp. 15-18. BO'N.
50. 'The Third Policeman' (pre-publication extract from the novel), *Transatlantic Review*, No. 25, 1967, pp. 78-83. FO'B.
51. 'Three Poems from the Irish', *Lace Curtain*, summer 1971, No. 4, pp. 46-7. MnaG.

C: Principal Unpublished Writings

1. 'The Insect Play'. Adapted from the play by Karel Čapek, 1943.
2. 'Thirst'. Broadcast by Radio Eireann, 1943.
3. 'The Boy from Ballytearim', 1961.

4. 'The Time Freddie Retired', 1962.
5. 'The Dead Spit of Kelly', 1962.
6. 'Flight', 1962.
7. 'The Man with Four Legs', 1962.
8. 'Slattery's Sago Saga'. An unfinished novel, 1965.
9. 'The Ideas of O'Dea'. 25 scripts for weekly television series, broadcast by Radio Telefis Eireann, September 1963 to March 1964.
10. 'Th' Oul Lad of Kilsalaher'. 13 scripts for weekly television series, broadcast by Radio Telefis Eireann, September to December 1965.

D: ABOUT BRIAN O'NOLAN

The following is a much-selected, chronological list of reviews and articles about Brian O'Nolan and his work.

1. Unsigned, 'Nest of Novelists', *Times Literary Supplement*, 18th March, 1939.
2. Frank Swinnerton, 'Right Proportions', *Observer*, 19th March, 1939.
3. Sean O'Faolain, 'Irish Gasconade', *John O'London's Weekly*, 24th March, 1939.
4. Unsigned, 'Irish Author's Experiment', *Irish Times*, 25th March, 1939.
5. Unsigned, 'Surrealist Sandwich: The Ireland of Fact, Fiction and the Pooka', *Glasgow Herald*, 30th March, 1939.
6. Maurice Richardson, 'Novels with and without Tears', *Books of the Month*, April 1939.
7. Humbert Wolfe, 'Books', *Sunday Referee*, 9th April, 1939.
8. Kate O'Brien, 'Fiction' *Spectator*, 14th April, 1939.
9. Edwin Muir, 'New Novels', *Listener*, 18th April, 1939.
10. Brian Vesey-FitzGerald, *The Field*, 29th April, 1939.
11. Dylan Thomas, 'Recent Fiction', *New English Weekly*, 18th May, 1939.
12. Anthony West, 'New Novels', *New Statesman and Nation*, 17th June, 1939.

13. Unsigned, 'A Literary Causerie: Irish Fantasy', *Northern Whig*, 10th July, 1939.

14. Unsigned, 'Thunder over Olympus', *Irish Times*, 16th October, 1939.

15. P.O'S., 'Books: *An Béal Bocht*', *The Bell*, Vol. III, No. 5, February 1942, pp. 405–6.

16. Gabriel Fallon, 'Copaleen O'Brien', *The Standard*, 7th February, 1943.

17. Richard Watts, 'Guest Critic' (review of *Faustus Kelly*), *The Bell*, Vol. V, No. 6, March 1943, pp. 482–7.

18. Unsigned, 'Eire's Columnist', *Time Magazine*, 23rd August, 1943.

19. Thomas Hogan (i.e. Thomas Woods), 'Myles na gCopaleen', *The Bell*, November 1946, Vol. XIII, No. 2, pp. 129–40.

20. Vivian Mercier, 'At Swim-Two-Birds', *Commonweal*, 27th April, 1951.

21. John V. Kelleher, 'Dublin's Joyce and Others', *Virginia Quarterly Review*, winter 1957, Vol. XXXIII, No. 1, pp. 132–5.

22. James Meenan (ed.), *Centenary History of the Literary and Historical Society, 1855–1955*, The Kerryman Ltd, Tralee, undated. References pp. 206, 230, 249–50, 251, 261, 262, 266, 312.

23. John Coleman, 'The Uses of Joyce', *Spectator*, 22nd July, 1960.

24. Quidnunc (ascribed, but probably Brian O'Nolan), 'A Visitation', *Irish Times*, 23rd July, 1960. (Reprinted as 'The Author in Person', *The Bookseller*, 8th August, 1960.)

25. Philip Toynbee, 'A Comic Heir of James Joyce', *Observer*, 24th July, 1960.

26. W. L. Webb, 'Laughter in Limbo', *Manchester Guardian*, 29th July, 1960.

27. Brendan Behan, 'Secret Scripture', *Irish Times*, 30th July, 1960.

28. John Jordan, 'The Saddest Book ever to come out of Ireland', *Hibernia*, 5th August, 1960.

29. V. S. Pritchett, 'Death of Finn', *New Statesman*, 20th August, 1960.

30. Michael Wharton, 'The Joycean Touch', *Daily Telegraph*, 16th September, 1960.

31. Benedict Kiely, 'Bells are ringing for a Work of High Genius', *Irish Press*, 11th November, 1961.

32. Paul Dehn, 'A Riot of Irishry', *Sunday Telegraph*, 12th November, 1961.

33. Unsigned, 'New Fiction', *The Times*, 16th November, 1961.

34. Anthony Burgess, 'Mister-piece', *Yorkshire Post*, 16th November, 1961.

35. Simon Raven, 'Cafard à la Crème', *Spectator*, 17th November, 1961.

36. W. L. Webb, 'Flann O'Brien's Misterpiece', *Manchester Guardian*, 17th November, 1961.

37. Terence de Vere White, 'Six Day Licence', *Irish Times*, 18th November, 1961.

38. Christine Brooke-Rose, 'Black, White and Grey Matter', *Observer*, 19th November, 1961.

39. John Gross, 'La Noia', *New Statesman*, 24th November, 1961.

40. Unsigned, 'Growing Up', *Times Literary Supplement*, 1st December, 1961.

41. Philip Larkin, 'Critics' Choice', *Manchester Guardian*, 15th December, 1961.

42. John Coleman, 'Keep Your Distance', *Queen*, 22nd December, 1961.

43. Elizabeth Jennings, 'New Novels', *Listener*, 28th December, 1961.

44. Unsigned, 'Region of the Mind', *Hibernia*, January 1962.

45. Maurice Kennedy, 'At Swim-Two-Birds', *Irish Times*, 5th November, 1962.

46. Iain Hamilton, 'Irish Irony Triple-Distilled', *Daily Telegraph*, 24th September, 1964.

47. John Coleman, 'A Quare Fellow', *Observer*, 4th October, 1964.

48. Elizabeth Smart, 'Books', *Queen*, 7th October, 1964.

49. Kay Dick, 'Disturbing Times', *Spectator*, 9th October, 1964.

50. B. A. Young, 'New Novels', *Punch*, 14th October, 1964.

51. Patrick Delaney, 'The Dalkey Sound', *Irish Times*, 22nd October, 1964.

52. Ian Sainsbury, 'The Best Comic Fantasy Since Tristram Shandy', *Sheffield Telegraph*, 24th October, 1964.

53. W. L. Webb, 'Flann Again', *Manchester Guardian*, 30th October, 1964.

54. Adrian Mitchell, 'The Bicycle', *New Statesman*, 4th December, 1964.

55. Tom MacIntyre, 'The Dalkey Archive', *Dublin Magazine*, spring 1965, p. 86.

56. S.C.F., 'Books', *The Kilkenny Review*, March 1965, pp. 140–1.

57. A. J. Leventhal, 'Paris Letter', *Irish Press*, 20th April, 1965.

58. Ian Sainsbury, 'Talking to Flann O'Brien', *Sheffield Telegraph*, 14th August, 1965.

59. Niall Carroll, 'Myles is now in full bloom', *Sunday Press*, 3rd October, 1965.

60. Niall Sheridan, 'Brian, Flann and Myles', *Irish Times*, 2nd April, 1966.

61. Niall Montgomery, 'An Aristophanic Sorcerer', *Irish Times*, 2nd April, 1966.

62. Mervyn Wall, 'The Man who hated only Cods', *Irish Times*, 2nd April, 1966.

63. Seamus Kelly, 'Scholar, Satirist and Wit', *Irish Times*, 2nd April, 1966.

64. Unsigned, 'Flann O'Brien, Novelist, 54 is Dead', *N.Y. Times*, 2nd April, 1966.

65. Peter Simple (i.e. Michael Wharton), 'Myles na Gopaleen', *Daily Telegraph*, 5th April, 1966.

66. John Wain, 'To Write for my own Race: The Fiction of Flann O'Brien', *Encounter*, July 1967, Vol. XXIX, pp. 71–85. (This article was later revised and expanded in *A House for Truth: Critical Essays*, Macmillan, 1972.)

67. Donagh MacDonagh, 'The Great Lost Novel', August 1967 (*unpublished*).

68. Frank McGuinness, 'Books', *Queen*, 1st September, 1967.

69. Mervyn Wall, 'A Nightmare of Humour and Horror', *Hibernia*, September 1967.

70. Benedict Kiely, 'Rare Roads to Hell', *Irish Times*, 2nd September, 1967.

71. Martin Seymour-Smith, 'Irishness', *Birmingham Post*, 2nd September, 1967.

72. Francis King, 'New Novels', *Sunday Telegraph*, 3rd September, 1967.

73. Julian Symons, 'Philosophy of a Comedian', *Sunday Times*, 3rd September, 1967.

74. Anthony Burgess, 'Surprise from the Grave', *Observer*, 3rd September, 1967.

75. Richard Lister (pseudonym), 'Three Stiff Policemen and a Soul called Joe', *Evening Standard*, 5th September, 1967.

76. John Raymond, 'Novels', *Punch*, 6th September, 1967.

77. Unsigned, 'Tall Talk', *Times Literary Supplement*, 7th September, 1967.

78. W. L. Webb, 'Terribly Funny', *Guardian*, 7th September, 1967.

79. Frederick Laws, 'A Hell of Confused Identity', *Daily Telegraph*, 7th September, 1967.

80. Kay Dick, 'Paradox and Poetry', *Spectator*, 15th September, 1967.

81. Augustine Martin, 'World within World', *Irish Press*, 23rd September, 1967.

82. Brigid Brophy, 'Preposterous', *Listener*, 28th September, 1967.

83. Unsigned, 'Fiction of the Month', *Guardian*, 27th October, 1967.

84. Benedict Kiely, 'Fun after Death', *N.Y. Times Book Review*, 12th November, 1967.

85. Timothy Hilton, 'Ireland's Great Cyclist', *New Statesman*, 8th December, 1967.

86. John Wain, 'Books of the Year', *Observer*, 10th December, 1967.

87. Unsigned, 'Inner Circles', *Time Magazine*, 26th January, 1968.

88. Thomas Kilroy, 'The Year in Fiction', *University Review*, spring 1968, pp. 112–16.

89. Bernard Benstock, 'Flann O'Brien in Hell; The Third Policeman', *Bucknell Review*, May 1968, pp. 67–78.

90. Personal Column: 'Some of the Best of Myles', *Spectator*, 16th August, 1968.

91. Christopher Salvesen, 'Irish Myles', *New Society*, 5th September, 1968.

92. Godfrey Fitzsimons, 'A Rattling Good Yarn', *Belfast Telegraph*, 6th September, 1968.

93. John Wain, 'Myles and Flann', *Observer*, 8th September 1968.

94. David Pryce-Jones, 'Irish Lawn', *Financial Times*, 12th September, 1968.

94. Henry Tube, 'It Goes without Synge', *Spectator*, 13th September, 1968.

96. Mervyn Wall, 'Mylestones', *Irish Times*, 14th September, 1968.

97. Unsigned, 'Mylestones', *Times Literary Supplement*, 19th September, 1968.

98. Michael Wharton, 'New Irish', *Punch*, 2nd October, 1968.

99. Patrick Boyle, 'At Whim—Few Surds', *Hibernia*, October 1968.

100. Richard Bennett, 'Wizard of Puns', *Sunday Telegraph*, 6th October, 1968.

101. Alexander Cockburn, 'Laughs O'Brine', *Listener*, 10th October, 1968.

102. Vivian Mercier, 'Witty Journalism by a (neglected) Irish Writer', *Book World*, 30th October, 1968.

103. Matthew Moulton, 'Irish Writers', *Scotsman*, 9th November, 1968.

104. Ian Sainsbury, '27 Years of Irish Laughter', *Morning Telegraph*, 16th November, 1968.

105. Benedict Kiely, 'The Best of Myles', *N.Y. Times Book Review*, 17th November, 1968.

106. Miles Kington, 'Myles out in Front', *The Times*, 7th December, 1968.

107. M. Raftery, 'Irish Parody at its Funniest', *Morning Star*, 19th December, 1968.

108. Florence O'Donoghue, 'Irish Spellbinder', *The Tablet*, 21st December, 1968.

109. Bernard Benstock, 'The Three Faces of Brian O'Nolan', *Eire-Ireland*, Vol. III, No. 3, autumn 1968, pp. 51–65.

110. Catherine Hughes, 'Discovering Flann O'Brien', *America*, 3rd May, 1969, pp. 523–5.

111. L. L. Lee, 'The Dublin Cowboys of Flann O'Brien', *Western American Literature*, Vol. IV, No. 3, fall 1969, pp. 219–25.

112. Bernard Cassen, 'Redécouverte de Flann O'Brien', *Le Monde*, 13th September, 1969.

113. Ivan del Janick, 'Flann O'Brien: The Novelist as Critic', *Eire-Ireland*, Vol. IV, No. 4, winter 1969, pp. 64–72.

114. John Wain, 'The Genius who Stayed at Home', *Le Monde*, 1st October, 1969.

115. Patrick Rafroidi, *L'Irlande: Littérature*, Armand Colin, Paris 1970, pp. 17, 140–2, 160.

116. Niall Sheridan, 'The World of Flann O'Brien', *R.T.E. Guide*, 13th November, 1970.

117. S. J. Perelman, 'Books of the Year', *Observer*, 20th December, 1970.

118. Clement Semmler, 'The Art of Brian O'Nolan', *Meanjin Quarterly*, Vol. 29, No. 4, December 1970, pp. 492–500.

119. William David Powell, *The English Writings of Flann O'Brien*, University Microfilm, Ann Arbor, Michigan 1971.

120. P. C. Power, 'Climbing the Mountain', *Dublin Magazine*, Vol. 9, No. 1, autumn 1971, pp. 68–73.